Letts EXPLORE

This book is to be returned on or before
the last date stamped below.

A *Letts* Literature Guide

First published 1997

Letts Educational
Aldine House
Aldine Place
London W12 8AW
0181 740 2266

Text © Chris Walton 1997

Typeset by Jordan Publishing Design

Text design Jonathan Barnard

Cover and text illustrations Hugh Marshall

Graphic illustration Hugh Marshall

Design © BPP (Letts Educational) Ltd

British Library Cataloguing in Publication Data
A CIP record for this book is available from the British Library

ISBN 1 85758 490 2

Printed and bound in Great Britain
by Nuffield Press, Abingdon

Letts Educational is the trading name of BPP (Letts Educational) Ltd

Contents

■ Plot synopsis

Henry V is about one of the most heroic incidents in English history: a war with France in which the English gained an unlikely victory, led by a great king who had changed out of all recognition from being a wild and reckless youth.

The play starts with the bishops of Canterbury and Ely expressing their concerns about a proposed bill, which, if passed, would strip the Church of more than half its possessions. Canterbury hopes to persuade the king to oppose the new law by providing money in support of a possible war with France. The king has claimed his right to the French throne, a right he has in the line of succession. The bishops also comment on the way that King Henry has changed. When he was younger he had a reputation for wild and debauched behaviour, mixing with disreputable friends in taverns in London. Now, he has become a model king with profound religious principles.

There is an ancient French law, the Salic law, which would appear to stand in Henry's way and prevent his claim to become king of France. However, Canterbury successfully argues that the law does not apply and so a war with France would be a just one. A French ambassador arrives with the reply of the Dauphin (the eldest son of the present king of France, Charles VI), and brings with him a joke gift of tennis balls for Henry. This is taken as a personal insult by the king, who warns the French what they will suffer at war. Before setting off to France, two other things happen: three traitors are uncovered and sentenced to death, and Falstaff, the king's old friend from his wild young days, dies. A sort of sub-plot is established as three old friends of Falstaff (and of the king), Pistol, Bardolph and Nym, are also setting off for war.

When the action switches to France, there is considerable disagreement about the threat of the English. The French king wants his defences to be reinforced, knowing that the English are a threat, from the defeats they have inflicted in the past. The Dauphin underestimates the English, still believing Henry to be the same wild character as he was in his youth. The Duke of Exeter arrives to present King Henry's claim. In a scroll that he gives the French, he presents the evidence that Henry is a descendent of Edward III, who was the grandson of a French king. Exeter also tells the French that Henry holds the Dauphin in contempt, and that he wants a speedy answer or war will follow. At the start of Act 3, Chorus tells us that all that the French king has offered is his daughter Katherine in marriage, with a dowry of insignificant dukedoms. The offer is rejected by the English and war commences.

At the siege of Harfleur, Henry spurs his men on to fight, recalling their ancestry as English warriors, although he does not succeed in motivating the likes of his old friends from the tavern. Pistol, Bardolph and Nym show that they are cowards, and they have to be driven on to fight by Captain Llewellyn, a Welshman who is a loyal servant and champion of the king's cause. There is another incident which calls into question the supposed national unity in the war: Llewellyn has a fierce argument with an Irish soldier called MacMorris, accusing him of being incompetent in the way he has set the mines at Harfleur.

Once Harfleur has been captured, Henry demands that the governor surrender or the consequences will be severe. He presents a terrifying account of what will happen if there is no surrender: he says that his soldiers will be uncontrollable. The Governor of Harfleur has received no support from the Dauphin, and so he must give in. The king intends to stop at Harfleur for one night and then to march on to Calais.

The action reverts briefly to the French king's palace at Rouen, where Princess Katherine is practising her English. The French lords describe how their nation is being mocked for the way it is having to give ground to the English army. The French king orders all his lords to defeat the English and bring Henry captive to Rouen.

Meanwhile in the English camp, Llewellyn is fooled into believing that Pistol has been a brave soldier whilst defending a bridge with Exeter, but then comes to realise his mistake. Pistol tries to intervene on behalf of his friend Bardolph, who is condemned to be hung for pilfering a cross from a church. Pistol is described by Gower as a false soldier; like many other rogues at the time, he knows how to sound brave, but is really a coward. The king confirms that Bardolph will be shown no leniency, and he is hung. Montjoy arrives, issues some threats and insults on behalf of the French, and tells Henry to name his ransom. Henry replies that, even though his army is weak, he intends to march on to Calais, and that the only ransom will be his own body.

The climax of the war takes place at Agincourt. The French nervously wait for the battle, bickering with each other, but are highly confident of victory as their army has such superiority of numbers. But King Henry is also nervous on the eve of the battle, and does the rounds of the camp in disguise, wearing the cloak of one of his lords, Sir Thomas Erpingham. First he meets Pistol, who praises the king and insults Llewellyn, and then he comes across three other soldiers, Bates, Court and Williams. Court says little, but the other two strike up a conversation about the way that the king is really responsible for the salvation or damnation of soldiers who go to their deaths in war. This leads to an argument and they end up exchanging gloves in order to recognise each other for a future challenge. Following this, in a soliloquy, Henry reflects on what it is to be a king.

Before the battle commences, there is a complacent mood of mockery in the French camp. The English are heavily outnumbered and their morale is low. The English feel the hopelessness of the situation, until a stirring speech from Henry in which he leads them confidently into battle. There is one more attempt by the French to get the English to name their ransom, in order to spare the deaths of so many soldiers, but Henry will not do this. He is ready for battle.

Incredibly, against all the odds, the French are defeated and the English suffer very few losses. The story of Agincourt is an epic 'David and Goliath' struggle, and victory is snatched largely thanks to King Henry's heroic leadership and powerful language, which inspires the men to bravery in battle. Somewhat predictably, however, Pistol does not behave heroically. He takes a French lord prisoner and threatens to cut his throat unless he is given a generous ransom. The French disgrace themselves by committing a war crime: they murder the English luggage boys. This enrages both Llewellyn and the king, who retaliates by ordering the execution of French prisoners. War is seen to be a terrible business.

Following his noble victory, the king plays a rather mean practical joke which leads Williams to challenge Llewellyn to a fight. Williams has been placed in a position in which he may have offended Henry, but the king gives him some money and the matter is smoothed over. Psalms and hymns of praise are sung to give thanks for the victory, and there is a jubilant return to England. Before the troops return, Llewellyn has one bit of unfinished business. Pistol has insulted his Welshness, so Llewellyn gets his own back by making Pistol eat raw leek! Pistol has not changed, and, dishonest to the last, he says that he will return to England wearing bandages on false wounds, swearing that he sustained the injuries at war.

In the final act, the scene shifts to the French king's palace at Troyes, where a peace treaty is concluded, following a passionate plea by the Duke of Burgundy, who describes the awful waste that has been caused by war in France. Henry woos the Princess Katherine, pretending not to have any of the skills or manners of a courtier. All of the English demands are granted by the French: Henry is named heir to the French throne and is offered Katherine's hand in marriage. Chorus has the final word, telling the audience that Henry VI, the king's son, subsequently loses France.

Medieval War

Medieval war involved heroic fighting and glorious victories,
but there were also instances of cowardice and retreat.
War caused terrible destruction and horrific death and injury.
Some men went to war to serve their king and country,
whereas others went for financial gain.

Henry V

King Henry V

When Shakespeare wrote *Henry V*, he wanted an epic subject to perform for Queen Elizabeth at a time when she had sent the Earl of Essex to crush a rebellion in Ireland. Chorus even refers to these events when he speaks directly to the audience about contemporary events in Act 5:

> 'Were now the general of our gracious empress,
> As in good time he may, from Ireland coming,
> Bringing rebellion broached on his sword'

The story of Henry V's heroic change, from wayward timewaster as a young prince, to noble Christian king who defeated the French at war, was the one Shakespeare chose. There is some historical evidence that the reign of Henry V was a life story fitting the idea of an epic struggle, but how true the eventual story was to the real life of Henry V is – as with all epic stories based on real lives – open to historical debate. What Shakespeare wanted to do was create an epic story that would satisfy the court of Queen Elizabeth and also satisfy a public who were full of nationalistic sentiments at the time. (Because of Essex's task in Ireland, there was probably a need for a story which was patriotic and nationalistic.) What better than the idea of an English king who had once fought a heroic struggle and won against a bitter enemy, defying all the odds!

To be a part of this epic story, the king needed to be an ideal Christian king. An epic had to teach moral values as well as tell a story. As a character, this king has a history. As Prince Hal, he has already appeared in *Henry IV*, *Parts i and ii*, and many of the changes in his personality have taken place before the start of the play (see the section on 'Conversion and reformation, p17). It was important that the prince of the past was no longer the king of the present.

What should an ideal king have been like? Shakespeare may have borrowed the idea from other Christian writers.

Try to find examples from the play for each of his virtues. He needed not only to be a Christian, but one who devoutly supported the Church. We hear in Act 1 that Henry is leaning towards the Church in its time of trouble. He had to be a well educated man, knowledgeable about theology (religious theory). He also had to show a capacity for justice and fairness, and never take personal revenge. Such a king needed to show self-control — an especially important point as Henry used not to show this as a younger man. In his dealings with other people, he would have accepted the counsel of wise men and mixed with ordinary people of a lower status, without being badly influenced by them. His mind would have been preoccupied with affairs of state, and most especially with its defence and advancement. This should have been a matter of great worry to Henry, causing him to stay awake at night. His kingdom had to be a harmonious state with everything working in an orderly manner, its subjects always obedient. Any rogues had to be banished or executed. The king needed to have the right sort of spirit for his position and not just enjoy the ceremony and trappings of power. Flattery had to be avoided. Christian kings could be compared with great warriors and leaders of the past, but they would have been superior to many of these, simply because they were Christians. The ideal king would have been aware of his responsibilities in war, knowing that he could be leading many to their deaths. Finally, such a king should have entered into marriage at some time in his life. The king's character is explored in greater detail in the section on **Themes and images**.

The characters from the tavern

Tavern characters

If you get a chance, try to read, or see, productions of *Henry IV*, *Parts i and ii*. In these plays, Shakespeare presents the character of Sir John Falstaff. This loveable rogue and villain from the tavern in London spent his time eating, drinking, gambling, swindling, womanising, thieving, swearing and telling dirty jokes! He is one of Shakespeare's finest comic creations. One reason why he is such an important character in the three plays (even though he does not appear in person in *Henry V*) is because the king, when he was Prince Hal, spent so much of his youth in the company of Falstaff, along with the other characters such as Bardolph, Pistol, Nym and Nell Quickly.

Towards the end of *Henry IV, Part ii*, King Henry IV dies and Prince Hal succeeds to the throne. Falstaff has been expecting favours and financial advancement when his old friend becomes king, but quite the opposite happens – he is rejected. Falstaff does not actually appear in *Henry V*, but there is news of his death. This is a moving moment, deliberately described in an emotional style. It is a moment of pathos. But it also breaks a link with the king's past. In Act 2, scene 4, we hear a rather muddled story from Nym and the Hostess that Falstaff has died repenting his sins. This seems to add to the epic ideas of the play as a symbol that even the greatest of rogues may have reformed.

The other characters from the tavern have not changed at all. Pistol, Nym and Bardolph undermine the idea of heroism and nobility at war. Pistol goes to war in order to make money. He admits this, and Gower at one point describes him as: 'a gull, a fool, a rogue, that now and then goes to the wars, to grace himself at his return into London under the form of a soldier'. What Gower is suggesting is that Pistol is like a lot of other soldiers from London: they would go to war and then make money out of bragging about their war exploits with false stories. He speaks in a way that makes himself appear to be a brave soldier, and he clearly does this successfully, as on one occasion he convinces the loyal Llewellyn.

In Act 4, scene 4, during the Battle of Agincourt, Pistol takes a French soldier prisoner and accepts a ransom of two hundred crowns, showing the prisoner mercy. He openly admits that he is doing exactly what he said he was going to war for: 'As I suck blood, I will some mercy show'. Because of his carefree and dishonest attitude, he comes into conflict with Llewellyn, whose character is full of honour. Significantly, it is Llewellyn's honour that Pistol insults and this is why he is punished. He is not used to having to deal with such morally upright characters, and in all his comments there are echoes of the past life that the king himself was once part of. In the end, almost nostalgically, Pistol is the only remaining survivor of the tavern days. He steadfastly stands out against reforming himself. The last we see of him is after he has been humiliated by Llewellyn; having eating his leek he says with great bravado that he will return to London, with false bandages: 'And swear I got them in the Gallia wars.'

Rogue and scoundrel as he is, what do we think of Pistol? Do we applaud Llewellyn's great sense of honour and condemn Pistol's mockery, or remain affectionate towards Pistol to the end, and perhaps by implication, regret what the king has lost from his carefree youth?

Bardolph and Nym do not survive. When we first meet them in Act 2, scene 1, they are just as raucous as Pistol, and in Act 2, scene 3 they contribute to the sad words spoken for Falstaff. Once at war, Nym, especially, reveals his cowardice: he cannot face moving forward in the siege of Harfleur, and, sadly, Bardolph is caught as a thief, for which he is executed. Like the death of Falstaff, his execution can be interpreted as a powerful moment in the drama. Is it another opportunity for the king to show the world that he has broken with his past? Do you feel sympathy for Bardolph, remembering his friendship with Prince Hal? It is also an incident which briefly suggests a theme of fortune (in the sense of fate, not money). Pistol says it is the fault of fortune that Bardolph is captured and is to be hung (he returns to his idea right at the end of his involvement in the play in Act 5, scene 1). In what senses are fortune and fate cruel to Bardolph and Pistol?

The play does not record Nym's death, but the Boy tells us that, like Bardolph, he too is hanged, and Pistol informs us that Doll Tearsheet has also died. It is very much the end of a world which gave audiences a great deal of entertainment and pleasure.

The French court

The Dauphin has failed to grasp the fact the Henry is a changed man. The tennis balls which he sends as a gift at the end of Act 1 are a contemptuous joke which backfires on the French. He thinks that such an insult befits the foolish reputation of Prince Hal, but has underestimated the reformation that has taken place in Henry's character. He is equally hot-headed on other occasions, although Shakespeare does not develop this personal rivalry between the two men in the way that he did in *Henry IV, Part i*, between Hal and Hotspur, a rebel lord. Indeed, the Dauphin is written out of the play altogether during Act 3, which diminishes his significance as a character. Sometimes directors find it appropriate to replace Bourbon with the Dauphin in Act 3, scene 8.

The French king, Charles, takes the threat of the English much more seriously. He remembers battles from the past and thinks it is wise to fortify against their advances. Yet in the French court generally there is a repeated impression of disunity and complacency. They never quite seem to agree about the English and they have differing views on King Henry. As Agincourt approaches they are scathing about their enemy, and through their insults, paint a picture of England as a damp, dismal, unsophisticated nation where the customs are quaint, the ale weak and the leadership poor. This then becomes complacency on a grand scale, so much so that they are sure the English troops will turn tail simply at the sight of the large French army. In the end, of course, when they are so dramatically defeated, their over-confidence turns to utter shame. Again, this is part of the epic struggle.

It is noticeable, however, that the French are honourable in defeat, and they call upon the Duke of Burgundy to negotiate a settlement (see the section on War in **Themes and images**).

Princess Katherine

Princess Katherine appears in two scenes, Act 3, scene 6 and Act 5, scene 2. When we first come across her, she is trying to learn some English words and struggling under the burden. Her discovery that some of the words sound the same as some rude French words could be interpreted as coyness, but on the other hand, she is anxious to continue her lesson! Later, when Henry is wooing her in Act 5, she again seems shy and reserved. She shows restraint when he tries to kiss her, first on the hand, and then, against all custom, on the lips.

There is no absolutely clear evidence as to what Shakespeare intended us to think of the princess. How would you interpret Katherine if you were producing the play? Is she simply a beautiful, coy princess, with no other attributes to her personality, or is there a self-conscious bashfulness in her style of behaviour? Why do you think Shakespeare has written her part in her native tongue? There is obviously a logical reason for this: she is learning English and can speak it only in a 'broken' tongue. But does it also allow her to hide her true self, so that she becomes rather seductive and coquettish as a result?

Llewellyn (sometimes spelled Fluellen)

Llewellyn

Apart from Pistol, this over-zealous Welsh captain is really the only other minor character in the play to be developed. He contrasts completely with the characters from the tavern. Whilst they are caricatures of a low life which the king has left behind, Llewellyn is, equally, a caricature of a devoted soldier and a loyal countryman. He exhibits to an absurd degree all the qualities associated with heroism, nobility and military strategy. He is a pedant (he has far too much to say for himself) and he is extremely fussy about matters such as discipline and punishment, which is of course why he conflicts with Pistol.

There are two ways in which Llewellyn is important to the themes of the play. His patriotic Welsh pride stresses the theme of national honour, and his obsessive worship of the king, whom he loves as a fellow Welshman, seems to add an extra focus to Henry's virtues. There is even a possibility that Llewellyn's virtues are more like an ideal monarch's than are the king's! Towards the end of the events at Agincourt, it is Henry who drops his guard and plays a practical joke, whilst Llewellyn stands firm as a man of honour and even temperament.

Chorus

Chorus

In other Shakespearean plays there are some devices used to present accounts of narratives, but this is the only play in which a Chorus is used before each act. One of the reasons was the grand nature of the events, which were very difficult to condense to a manageable timescale in the theatre. Chorus asks the audience to extend its imagination in order to follow the mighty and extensive events of war.

He adds a tone of realism, so that the audience can be helped to imagine the departures, the sailings, the preparations and actions of battle scenes. He frequently speaks of these events in a grand, eloquent and poetic style, reinforcing the epic, poetic structure of the work. He apologises to the audience lest the theatre is unable to present the events as they need to be shown, although some critics have suggested that this could be tongue-in-cheek, with Chorus really drawing attention to the play's qualities as opposed to its shortcomings. Notice also the way that Chorus is a real fan of King Henry. He constantly depicts him as a great hero, almost as if this is the official interpretation.

There is just one way in which you might want to question whether there is a more deceptive purpose to Chorus. He does on occasions seem to exaggerate the events in a form of poetry known as hyperbole. In Act 2, for example, he says: 'honour's thought reigns solely in the breast of every man'.

Is this really the case as the play unfolds in the next act? In modern times we might use the word 'propaganda' to describe some of his language. Propaganda is the art of bending the truth so that nations at war can feel confident and morale is kept high. It is a way of *misrepresenting* the truth, without necessarily telling outright lies.

■ Themes and images in *Henry V*

War

War

All aspects of war are present in the play. War is a triumphant event, provoking values such as patriotism and heroism, loyalty and courage. These views are best expressed during some of the speeches at the Battle of Agincourt. In Act 4, scene 3, Henry leads his men on by an appeal to their honour and their manhood, and the French feel 'shame, and eternal shame, nothing but shame!' in defeat. Part of the English honour stems from patriotism, but it is also due to a love of God and a feeling of the righteousness of just war. Look at the spiritual celebration at the end of the war in the words spoken by the king and Llewellyn in Act 4, scene 8. The victory is marked by the singing of a psalm and a hymn, *Non nobis* and *Te Deum*.

Although noble heroism and great courage are the war values for the majority, there is also evidence of cowardice in the behaviour of Pistol, Nym and Bardolph, so much so that the Boy speaks out against it and says how disillusioned he is by what he has witnessed. As has already been discussed, Pistol's actions also show a mercenary side to war (a mercenary is somebody who attempts to make money from the activities of war).

As well as these basic values, the play also provides some horrific descriptions of war and thoughts about its consequences, as well as issues of responsibility. We gain insight into its destructiveness and waste. It is seen as an unstoppable force, ruining lives and nature. The king is the first to raise this theme in Act 1, scene 2:

'We charge you in the name of God take heed,
For never two such kingdoms did contend
Without much fall of blood, whose guiltless drops
Are every one a woe, a sore complaint
'Gainst him whose wrongs give edge unto the swords
That makes such waste in brief mortality.'

Animal imagery is used to show the horrors of war. In Act 2, scene 4, Exeter describes hungry war opening 'his vasty jaws', and the king tells his men to 'imitate the action of the tiger' at the siege of Harfleur. He also uses the image of a storm – 'when the blast of war blows in our ears' – to stress its strength.

In Act 3, scene 4, Henry explains how soldiers can become uncontrollable. They will commit acts of crime and violation on a frightening scale, once let loose. He describes soldiers in this violent state as 'blind and bloody'. Daughters, mothers, infants and fathers will be howling and screaming at the frenzied brutality they would have to endure. These images of butchery, waste and desolation are further developed in Burgundy's speech in Act 5, scene 2. He contrasts the beauty and creativity of peace with the savagery and unnaturalness of war, during which land is laid to waste and men do not prosper. His is a vision of disorder: a world in which nature loses its beauty, the land its fertility and humans their dignity. During a period of war, people become savages and give up the pursuit of 'sciences' – education and knowledge.

The play presents a kind of documentary of war. Chorus describes the excited preparations, the efforts to arm the country, the fears and anguish suffered by the English army on the night before the battle, and, of course, the triumphant return. As well as the heroic deeds of brave soldiers, we see terrible offences, which in modern times would be termed war crimes, the worst of which is the murder of the luggage boys. We gain an impression of the shame and despair involved in defeat, and we are shown the sheer terror of individuals when Williams speaks his thoughts and when Pistol captures a French soldier.

As well as war, the play is also about peace, evident during the negotiations of the final act. Peace is not presented as a sentimental idea: it is a matter of difficult negotiation leading to a union of the interests of the two nations, expressed in a tone of reconciliation. As Chorus indicates in his final speech, however, this was a fragile concept in the medieval world.

Conversion and reformation

Conversion

The fact that the king has changed from being a riotous youth to a truly Christian adult plays an important part. The king himself uses every opportunity to show his new character; he is reported by others as being a changed man, but the French never come to terms with this and underestimate his reformation. His conversion has led the king to become not simply a devoted Christian but an ideal, a shining example in the virtues of Christianity and kingship. This is obviously exaggerated for the purposes of the epic story.

In Act 1, scene 1, Canterbury identifies the moment the king began to change as when his father died. The 'wildness' that he had lived with in his youth seemed to die along with his father: 'at that very moment, consideration like an angel came'.

It was a sudden, profound and divine change. His body became a 'paradise' as he took on the virtues of Christianity and left his idleness behind him. He became a 'scholar'; he could discuss matters of theology and he turned his attention fully to all the important matters in the affairs of state. The most important aspect of his change was shown in the way that he used his time. Whereas in his youth he had been known to fill his hours with 'riots, banquets, sports', once reformed he retired to study and gave his time to the proper functions of a thoughtful man of state.

Ely's image of a 'strawberry growing underneath the nettle' suggests that Henry always had the potential to change, but there are various possible interpretations of his reformation. Are you convinced by the presentation of an ideal Christian? Do you think, as some have suggested, that he is shrewd, and knows exactly how to say the right things at the right time in order to sound convincing, like a politician? Are there still aspects of his youth which remain in his character?

Think again about the part that the tavern characters play in constantly reminding us of Henry's reformation.

Religion

Religion

A careful reading of the play should show you the contrast between the rudeness and ill-breeding of the French and the constant reminders of unity, honour and righteousness amongst the English. The sort of disunity and dishonour that increasingly befall the French seems to suggest that as part of the epic struggle, we are witnessing some sort of war between good and bad. The play opens with Churchmen describing the new ways of the king, now a man of God.

Go through the play as you are getting to know it and identify how often this is borne out. Henry frequently identifies with the causes of his God, as if they were leaders of the same war. A medieval king was seen as a person having the authority of God on earth, as if he were next in line, a sort of earthly deputy to the Lord.

As he awakens to his task of kingship, and as he grows into it, Henry seems to gain more and more inspiration from God and it is this that, so he says, drives on his powers and offers him such moral courage. Certainly there are moments when we can find him returning to his old ways, but these can be interpreted as very natural human characteristics – as he says in Act 4, scene 1: 'in his' (a king's) 'nakedness, he appears but a man'. But setting these moral lapses aside, it is hard not to feel his sincerity as a religious man, most notably in the speech when he prays directly for help the night before the battle (Act 4, scene 2). By this time there is an evident difference between the mocking, cynical tone of the French and the honourable, unified and earnest tone of the English under their dedicated king.

As a theme in the play, religion is straightforward. There is none of the questioning of life hereafter that plagues Hamlet, and no great insight into the controlling powers of spiritual life that haunt King Lear. Religion here is part of the medieval ideal: a force of good, involving the idea that God's word and code is there to be obeyed. As this happens to the English, under such a reformed Christian king, so they defeat the French, whose disunity appears to represent a lack of righteousness.

Conspiracy

Conspiracy

The conspirators who are unmasked in Act 2 touch a raw nerve, and their dramatic plot to bring about the death of the king is a terrible act of evil. But the reason why it is such an important part of the play is because it provides Henry with a wonderful opportunity, however it hurts him personally, to show his new character. In his indictment speech in Act 2, scene 2, lines 76–141, he uses language almost as a rehearsal for the demands that will be placed upon him later, when abroad in France. It is a highly moralistic speech, full of contrasts in ideas and images, setting out very clearly that there are two paths to be chosen in life; one of righteousness and one of sin.

He uses the imagery of monsters and beasts, of devils and fiends, to describe his one-time friends. Their actions are like the fall of man, all the worse when they appeared to the world as honest and scrupulous. Henry also takes it upon himself to 'weep for them', as if what they have done is to return the world to a state of sin and damnation. What other 'conspiracies' are there in the play?

Leadership and rhetoric

Rhetoric

What qualities of leadership can you discover in Henry? He is constant and determined, he inspires others, he does not flinch from the use of authority or the needs of courage and bravery in battle. He is inspiring and noble. But how does he achieve these qualities? Look carefully at his use of rhetoric. Rhetoric is that kind of speech which is intended to be effective and powerful due to its structure. Sometimes we listen to the diction as much as to the meaning, we discover flourishes of great poetry and moments of strong emotion in what is said, so that we react, rather than consider the meaning of the ideas.

That is not to say that there are no reflective moments in the language: Act 4, scene 1 is an extremely introspective part of the play, but generally, Henry's speeches are structured to impress and persuade, to inspire and enthuse. Look carefully at the key moments, the times when Henry stirs his men into action or changes the course of history. Consider the way he mixes the images of sea, storm and wild animals at Harfleur (Act 3, scene 1). Look again at his strong alliteration and the metaphorical use of monsters, as he charges the Governor to open the gates of Harfleur in Act 3, scene 4. Then study closely the nuances of emotion, the directness of his personal voice, his passion for honour and valour through the love of all men as one brotherhood in Act 4, scene 3. Henry stands alongside Mark Anthony as one of Shakespeare's finest rhetoricians.

■ Text commentary

Act 1
The prologue

Presenting a play about a war with France will not be easy. The Chorus calls for help from the goddess of poetry in order to represent the scenes. He tells the audience that they will need great powers of imagination in order to behold the events of the play, transferred from a vast battlefield to the theatre.

'Can this cockpit hold the vasty fields of France?'

Chorus

The Chorus speaks before the beginning of each act. Although there are uses of a chorus in other Shakespearean plays, this is the only one in which the part is a large one. The use of Chorus contributes to the epic form of the play – a stirring legend in which the speech and the actions need to be presented on a grand scale. In his first speech, Chorus apologises to the audience for using 'flat unraised spirits' to bring out the turbulence of war. The words alert us immediately to some of the play's most powerful war themes. 'Harry' (King Henry) is likened to the warlike Roman god of war, Mars, and we are asked to imagine the two nations of England and France parting asunder 'the perilous narrow ocean'. It is clearly going to be an epic drama about war on a grand scale.

Act 1, scene 1

The Bishops of Canterbury and Ely are anxious about a proposed bill which, if passed, would force the Church to give up the majority of its possessions. The bill would ruin the Church. They take comfort in the fact that the king has become a reformed character after his father's death, and is now a true man of the Church. Canterbury has heard that the king may not be sympathetic towards those who want to pass the bill against the Church, and has offered money from the Church to help the king claim the throne of France. The Church will support the war. We hear that a French ambassador has arrived with an answer to the claim.

Reformation

Religion

Act 1, scene 1 serves a number of purposes. The action of the play fits into a classic historical mould. The Church is under threat in difficult times at home and the bishops are glad of the opportunity to divert attention away from the forthcoming bill. There is an important description of the king. He has spent a misguided youth, as presented in two earlier plays, *Henry IV, Parts i and ii*, but he has since reformed. It is interesting to look at the language used by Canterbury to describe the king's transformation. Epic literature often contains exaggerated language. We hear that Henry's body is 'as a paradise... t'envelop and contain celestial spirits'.

'...blessed in the change'

Study closely the two speeches spoken by Canterbury from lines 24 to 59.

Henry V

You can gain insight into the king's new character from what Canterbury says. It is important to understand the extreme change that Henry has undergone. We hear that, in his youth (when he was known as Prince Hal), he mixed with bad company, filling up his time with 'riots, banquets, sports', and he was not noted for the sorts of things that would have prepared him for kingship. He was a sociable young man who could not keep himself away from public places, in particular taverns. Later in the play we are going to meet some of the characters with whom he kept company. Unlike the king, however, they have not reformed.

Conversion

Canterbury describes Henry's character now as being full of grace. He stresses the way that he has become a complete man of God, more appropriate to the requirements of a good king. In some ways, the play is a study of the nature of kingship, and this is the first opportunity we get to understand what is required of an ideal Christian king. To summarise what Canterbury says: as well as having become devout in religion, he now understands well the affairs of state and politics and the tactical needs of war and he uses speech eloquently (in 'sweet and honeyed sentences') to lead his subjects.

'In regard of causes now at hand'

Canterbury knows that the bill against the Church would have serious

Religion

consequences if it were passed. Lines 11 to 18 tell us exactly what the Church would lose. He has been clever, however, in offering a considerable sum of money to support the coming war with France:

> '...a greater sum
> Than ever at one time the clergy yet
> Did to his predecessors part withal.'

So, although there have been tensions at home, it appears likely that court and Church will unite with one cause abroad. The tension develops as we hear that the French ambassador has arrived. He will give France's reply to King Henry's claim to the French throne.

Act 1, scene 2

The king asks Canterbury to explain what effect the Salic Law has on his claim to the throne of France. He warns Canterbury that his words will be very important; the court will take his advice. Canterbury presents two arguments: firstly, that the Salic Law does not apply in France (it is applicable only in Germany); secondly, although the law states that nobody can come to the throne if they are descended from a female line, there have been examples of this happening. Thirdly, Canterbury quotes from the Bible to justify a female line of inheritance. Henry is persuaded, but recognises a danger in the rear from Scotland, so the country must also be defended at home.Canterbury supports King Henry by stressing the importance of the division of labour, comparable to the workings of a beehive. The king shows his determination: he will conquer France, or die. The French ambassador arrives, with an insulting gift from the Dauphin: he gives the king a set of tennis balls. This enrages Henry, who insults the Dauphin with a display of clever wit and strong warnings.

'...what you speak is in your conscience washed As pure as sin with baptism'

Henry V

The king asks Canterbury to explain the just cause for his claim to the French throne. He asks in a very pious tone of voice, reminding us of his conversion to religion. He is impressive in the way he presents his demands, as war is a serious business. The result of Canterbury's words is that men will 'drop their blood' if the country is led into war.

The Salic Law

This is complicated, and Canterbury has to present his arguments in a long-winded way. Why is it so important for him and the Church that he should persuade the king of a just cause for war? Is war in his interests? You will need to read Canterbury's speech a few times in order to understand the arguments. You should find the following lines of argument in what he says: the only barrier to Henry's claim to the French throne is an ancient law derived from Pharamond, a legendary king from the eastern part of France. This law states that no king can succeed to the throne if he is descended from a female line (Henry's association with France is that his great-great grandmother, Isabella, was daughter to a French king). Firstly, Canterbury argues, the law does not even apply in France, as Salic land is in Germany. Then he argues that, in any event, there are many examples of French kings descended from females, so the law cannot be applied and the French are using it wrongly. In a grave and serious tone of speech, he concludes by quoting from the Bible where it is written in the Book of Numbers: 'when the man dies, let the inheritance descend unto the daughter'.

'....proportions to defend Against the Scot...'

War

What do you make of Henry's thoughts about defending the country against a rearguard attack from the Scots? Notice that, as well as being a strong Christian king, who wants to know that he has just cause for a bloody war with France, he is also tactically very aware of other consequences. A picture is beginning to build up of a highly capable king – a contrast indeed to the carefree prince he was in his youth. This part of the play also brings out its own sense of history. The king, Canterbury and Westmorland all refer to events of the past. In previous wars with France, the Scots have made fearful advances and they are presented now as a terrifying force, through a series of vivid images.

Two central images: 'music' and 'the honey bees'

Exeter describes the harmony of government needed to attack and defend as being 'like music'. Canterbury follows this with a longer, extended image in which he compares the state of man to the work of 'honey bees'. This is an important image, as it stresses the unity of the nation. Canterbury basically says that, just as the bees do, all parts of the nation work in different ways to one purpose. What do you think of Canterbury as a character? Unquestionably, his words have motivated the king and the nobles, but for what other reasons might he have spoken so convincingly?

'Now are we well resolved'

Henry V

The king is determined to go to war. Notice how he calls upon God and his noblemen to succeed. He begins to show some of the qualities of leadership and determination that eventually win the war for England: he will either rule over France, or die. Can you see how the audience is beginning to sense the epic heroism in the themes of the play?

King Henry: 'What treasure, uncle?' *Exeter:* 'Tennis balls, my liege.'

The mocking gift of the tennis balls from the Dauphin is the first indication

Henry V

that the French have underestimated King Henry. The gift is brought to England to mock the man Henry is still assumed to be, a wild and foolish youth.

Henry retorts with a speech of brilliant wit, perhaps angered because he has been personally insulted. He uses a series of puns and images drawn from tennis, hunting and war, sending the ambassador back to France with a strong warning that they will meet their match if they think they are dealing with a weak king. Consider how the repeated use of the word 'mock' towards the end of the speech is designed to provoke terror and fear in the minds of the French.

The scene ends with yet another reminder from the king that he has a religious cause, and will lead the country to war with God on his side.

Self-test Questions Act 1

Uncover the plot

Delete two of the three alternatives given, to find the correct plot. Beware possible misconceptions and muddles.

Chorus calls for help from another writer/the actors/the god of poetry to help present the action of the play. He says that the play will be about a war between two great men/prime ministers/monarchs and as the war takes place the audience will have to imagine the soldiers/cavalry/longbow-men moving about the stage. Canterbury is worried about a proposed law/coup/summons which will strip the Church of its wealth, and when Ely asks him what he has done about it/how to prevent it/if it is bound to happen, Canterbury is able to praise the king's style/appearance/goodness. He outlines the ways in which the king has governed/changed/argued and indicates that the Church is willing to support war with France financially/agree to a new tax system/call for the king's abdication. The king asks Canterbury for reasons why the war with France might be just/worth the risk/agreeable to the people, and Canterbury backs it up with an explanation of the Salic Law, which states that there could be no heir to the French throne from an only child/an unmarried prince/a female line. The king says that they will go to war with France, but must take care of their rear/weapons/soldiers, in order to avoid further danger. Canterbury supports the war effort in a speech comparing the government of the country with mother nature/a fast flowing stream/honey bees. An ambassador from France arrives with a message from the Dauphin, that the king is still too juvenile/a force to be reckoned with/an honoured monarch. He has also brought a dowry/treaty/mocking gift. When he receives this, the king retorts with a display of wit/sits down and weeps/suggests a new treaty to keep the peace. He tells his lords to retreat to the country/prepare for war/take a holiday.

Who? What? Why? When? Where? How?

1   What should the 'cockpit' (theatre) hold?
2   What needs to 'be crammed within this wooden O'?
3   Why are Ely and Canterbury worried about the future?
4   What was 'never noted' in the young Henry?
5   Why should the Salic Law not stand in the way of the king's claim to the French throne?
6   How does Canterbury suggest that the king should defend against the Scots at home?
7   When the messenger from France presents the king with the gift of tennis balls, what does Henry succeed in doing with his language?
8   What does Henry warn the French he will do in France?
9   To whom does Henry appeal for help?
10   Where will he 'chide this Dauphin'?

Who said that, and to whom?

1 'the king is full of grace, and fair regard.'
2 '...his addiction was to courses vain.'
3 'And so the prince obscured his contemplation
Under the veil of wildness...'
4 '...what you speak is in your conscience washed
As pure as sin with baptism.'
5 ' –No woman shall succeed in Salic land – '
6 'May I with right and conscience make this claim?'
7 'Your brother kings and monarchs of the earth
Do all expect that you should rouse yourself...'
8 'But there's a saying, very old and true,'
9 'I this infer,
That many things, having full reference
To one consent, may work contrariously.'
10 'this mock of his
Hath turned his balls to gun stones,'

Explain the importance of:

1 A man divided into a thousand parts.
2 An hour-glass.
3 The death of King Henry IV.
4 The strawberry beneath the nettle.
5 Germany.
6 A great-uncle.
7 The tide into a breach.
8 Honey bees.
9 A nimble galliard.
10 The tun opened.

Act 2

Chorus describes the patriotic preparations for war. The nation is enthusiastic in its support for King Henry, the Christian king. Unfortunately, three noblemen have been traitors and are involved in a conspiracy with France, in return for money. Chorus describes how the scene must shift to Southampton, where the English troops will depart for France, and where the traitors will be put to death.

'Now all the youth of England are on fire'

The lively style with which Chorus describes the preparations for war

War

expresses a mood of patriotic enthusiasm in the country. Here, we recognise the epic nature of the play, in which *hyperbole* (extreme exaggeration) is used in order to give the impression that the country is totally supportive of the king. What impression of him do you get when he is described as 'the mirror of all Christian kings'?

This is a stirring, patriotic speech. England is described as a 'model to inward greatness' and there is a tone of utter contempt for the actions of the traitors,

Cambridge, Scroop and Gray, who have 'confirmed conspiracy with France'. Chorus also serves a theatrical role. He explains to the audience how they can be transported across the sea in order to witness the events of the war, without offending 'one stomach with our play'. Again, Shakespeare attempts to deal with the difficult problem of helping his audience to imagine these events, which are on a grand scale.

Act 2, scene 1

Before moving to Southampton, the action in this scene is interrupted by a return to 'The Boar's Head', a tavern in London where the king spent much of his time in younger days. Pistol has married Nell Quickly, who had promised herself to Nym. When Pistol and his wife arrive in the tavern there is a huge argument between Pistol and Nym and they draw their swords to fight. Bardolph tries to keep the peace. The Boy arrives with the news that Sir John Falstaff is very ill. Falstaff is a lord who has led a life of debauchery: drinking, gambling, and spending time with prostitutes. As Prince Hal, the king knew him well and spent a lot of time with him, but when he became king, Henry rejected Falstaff. The Hostess calls for them to come quickly to Falstaff, as he is nearing the end.

'...it will be thought we keep a bawdy house...'

To appreciate the importance of these minor characters in the play, it is important to understand some of the events of the first two plays in the sequence, *Henry IV, Parts i and ii*. These bawdy characters were once Henry's companions. He may have changed, becoming more statesmanlike and noble, but the characters from the tavern are still the same. There are different views on the rights and wrongs of the king's involvement with the tavern in his youth. It could be interpreted as a waste of time when he should have been preparing for the serious business of state and of becoming a king one day. Or it could be seen as a spell in the university of life, putting him in touch with the real people.

The argument between Pistol and Nym is bawdy, with lots of sexual puns. They observe no decorum in the way they speak to each other and they are strong with their insults. Indeed, Pistol speaks with such venom, repeatedly using the word 'and' as he builds up his insults, that Nym even thinks he is being bewitched with a chant of the devil!

'Come, shall I make you two friends?'

The incidents in this scene are not independent of the main action. These men will also have to go to war in France, and so Bardolph tries to get them to calm down, aware that they must all go together to fight. Can you see another possible idea in the play here? Is there as much unity amongst people in the country as Chorus has led us to believe? In the event, Pistol relaxes and actually shows quite a lot of friendship towards Nym, although we suspect another motive for his desire for 'brotherhood': he wants to make a profit from the war and perhaps feels he can achieve this better if he is not at loggerheads with his old friend. Pistol buys Nym's forgiveness with the promise of a 'noble' (worth six shillings and eight pence), and they make up.

'The king hath run bad humours on the knight'

Although Falstaff does not appear in this play, it is important to bear in mind his past role. We associate him with the king's youth as a wayward prince – they were great friends – and now we hear that, because of his rejection by the king, Falstaff is dying with a broken heart. There are implications here of important questions and ideas connected with Falstaff's approaching death. Has the king been unfair in rejecting him, or has he done what is only right and proper for the sake of the country? In your opinion, does the rejection of Falstaff present the king in a good or a poor light? The Boy and the Hostess are clearly upset by the news, as they call the others to him in his deathbed.

Act 2, scene 2

Westmorland describes the falseness of the traitors. The three men appear, in what they say, to be excessively loyal to the king. Henry orders the release of a prisoner who has been detained for insulting him after too much drinking, but the traitors argue that this shows too much leniency. Without realising it, they have set themselves a trap. Henry gives them their papers, but these indict them for the crime they have committed. In a long speech, Henry then condemns them, legally, morally and spiritually. He is particularly upset at the actions of Lord Scroop, who was a friend of his.

Traitors

How does Shakespeare succeed in showing the treacherous characters of Cambridge, Scroop and Gray? Think about the way that their language suggests an appearance of dutiful and loving speech and also how they praise the king's leadership. You should be able to detect how false this is. Consider the style of their language. What do we learn about their attitudes in lines such as Scroop's 'No service shall with steeled sinews toil'? What effect is made by all the alliteration on the 's' sounds? Does it make you think that Scroop is exaggerating his devotion to the king? Is he playing at being a loyal subject?

Look at the trap the traitors fall into as they so readily condemn the man whom the king wants to free in an act of mercy. In the way that they condemn him to his punishment, are they really arguing for a lack of mercy to be shown to them?

'For this revolt... is like another fall of man'

The incident with the traitors is interesting for the way that Henry reacts to

Henry V

it. In his long indictment (condemnation) speech, he uses *rhetoric*. His techniques and devices are a deliberate attempt to have an effect on his listeners.

Henry takes the chance to impress upon those around him in the court that he is strong and ruthless and can therefore be trusted as the king. His language is strong. He uses animal and monster imagery to describe the traitors; he stresses the way that he loved and honoured these men, and thus he has been cruelly betrayed. But by far the strongest feature of his language is the religious condemnation of the traitors. This is important, linking with other parts of the play in which we can assess his development as a strong Christian king. Look carefully at the numerous references he makes to damnation, hell, the devil and the fall of man. The traitors had tried to appear noble and religious, loyal and devoted. The truth was different.

As always with any attempt to interpret Shakespeare precisely, there is no clear agreement on Henry's motives in this scene. What do you think he intends? Is he genuinely upset by the deception of the traitors? Or is it more the case that he uses the opportunity to reveal that he is now a very strong Christian king, capable of ruthless punishment and religious correctness?

Act 2, scene 3

In 'The Boar's Head' tavern in London, the Hostess is describing Falstaff's death to Bardolph, Pistol, Nym and the Boy. Pistol says farewell to the Hostess as they have to leave for war in France.

'... as cold as any stone'

Although Falstaff appeared in *Henry IV, Parts i and ii*, he does not take part in

Tavern characters

Henry V at all. Shakespeare has his death reported by the Hostess. It is a strong moment in the play. Falstaff was a great friend and *mentor* (leader, teacher) of the king's when he was younger. Elizabethan audiences would have known and loved the character of Falstaff from the earlier plays. He was a popular character, larger than life, a sort of loveable villain – debauched, yes, but comic and harmless!

The Hostess describes his actual death in a touching and emotional style, although rather comically, she gets many of her words wrong! She says that he was crying out for God, and Nym has heard that he 'cried out of sack' (spoke out against the evils of drink). The way in which the Hostess confuses the word 'incarnate' for carnation makes their grief all the more touching and it is also rather distressing how they try to agree whether or not he died a Christian death. It is a rare scene even for Shakespeare, a scene of pure grief on the stage.

One other point worth noting is the way that Shakespeare *juxtaposes* (sets side by side) two different kinds of worlds: the world of the new king at court, a world of Christian values and power; against the world which the king as Prince Hal used to frequent. There is a constant reminder of his past life.

'Let us to France... the very blood to suck'

War

The play as a whole is about the war with France. We know from Chorus that 'now sits expectation in the air'. It is much more than the story of the noble king and his lords and earls. The characters from 'The Boar's Head' prepare to go to France, as do the nobles. Pistol's parting words introduce a theme of *avarice* (a love of money) at war, which will contrast throughout the campaign with the more noble and heroic war themes. Carefully follow the progress of Pistol and Bardolph through France. How would you assess their attitudes to war?

Act 2, scene 4

This scene takes place in France, in the king's palace at Rouen. The French king orders his dukes to reinforce the defences of the towns for the coming battles with England. Earlier defeats at the hands of the English have taught him a lesson. Although the Dauphin agrees that France should prepare for war, he feels they should have no fear of the English because of the poor reputation of King Henry. He argues this view further with the Constable, who is convinced that King Henry has changed. The French king reminds them that King Henry is a descendent of the Black Prince, and therefore must be feared.

The Duke of Exeter and other ambassadors arrive from England and Exeter sets out the English demands. The French king must give up his crown to King Henry, who has a right to it through his ancestry, as he is descended from Edward III. Exeter hands over a family tree in a scroll to prove to the French that the claim is legal. When asked what will happen if the claim is not met, Exeter describes the terrible consequences of the war that will follow. He also informs the Dauphin that King Henry holds him personally in contempt after receiving the tennis balls. Finally, he describes the way that Henry has changed. To all this, the French king replies that he will provide his answer the next day. We learn that Henry and the English troops have already landed in France.

'...our defences'

Each of the characters in the French court takes a differing view of what to do. The king, who is sometimes played as an old and sick man, thinks that

French court

France should be strongly fortified, as he fears the English. He recalls some of the earlier battles which the English have won on French soil. The Dauphin, on the other hand, mocks the English. Whilst he agrees that it is probably wise to prepare their defences, he says 'let us do it with no show of fear'. He still has an impression that England is 'idly kinged'. The Constable has heard, to the contrary, that King Henry has changed. One of the advantages of hearing his speech about the English king is that we get another view of Henry. What impressions of Henry does his speech give?

In this scene we have our first glimpse of the way that the French squabble amongst themselves and also how prone they are to getting things wrong. The Dauphin comes across as arrogant when he says:"'tis best to weigh the enemy more mighty than he seems'.

He remains arrogant throughout the play, and the French often appear quarrelsome and divided. Here we notice that the Dauphin is already underestimating King Henry. Also, memories of the earlier battles that the French have lost against the English should perhaps have warned them of the likely courage and bravery of the English this time.

'he bids you then resign your crown and kingdom'

The tone of Exeter's speech is formal and statesmanlike. Notice the confident way he sets out King Henry's demands. The legal justification comes about because Henry is the great grandson of Edward III, who in turn was the grandson of Philip V, a king of France. The idea of a just war has already been discussed; here, Exeter uses another opportunity to stress the justness of the cause.

'this hungry war'

The formal tone of Exeter's speech, in which he sets out Henry's demands,

War

helps to stress the gravity of the situation. He follows this with a threatening tone in which he describes, through the use of some strong and vivid imagery, how terrible the ensuing war will be. War will be a frightening alternative if the demands are not met. Bear in mind that the audience would be supporting the English claims, because the justness of the cause has been established.

'Scorn and defiance; slight regard, contempt'

As well as the formal demands, Exeter has one further point to make: he has brought a personal message from Henry to the Dauphin. Exeter's tone of speech has changed again towards the end of the scene. He reports Henry's

Henry V

bitter contempt for the Dauphin following the insult of the tennis balls. The Dauphin displays a stubborn and angry attitude in return, saying that even if the French king gives in to the demands, he personally will remain an enemy to Henry.

One of the things that this exchange stresses is the change that has come over King Henry. Most of the Dauphin's contempt arises from his prejudice that the English king is still a man of 'youth and vanity'. Exeter tries to put him right on this matter, using a phrase which is meant to describe Henry's nobility: 'Now he weighs time even to the utmost grain'.

What do you think of the Dauphin's attitude towards Henry? Is he being foolish?

Self-test Questions Act 2

Uncover the plot
Delete two of the three alternatives given, to find the correct plot. Beware possible misconceptions and muddles.

Nym is angry that Nell Quickly is drunk/dead/married and as a result he praises/insults/jokes with Pistol. The Boy tells the other characters from the country/tavern/court that their old friend Falstaff is very ill/has gone to war/has been left some money. They regret that Falstaff has had his heart broken/been stripped of his rank/been imprisoned by the king.

Meanwhile, the king faces a problem. Cambridge, Scroop and Gray have become thieves/violent/traitors and they must be sentenced accordingly. Before he punishes them Henry agrees to pardon another man/wait for a longer trial/set them free. When he speaks to the three men he compares their actions to the signs of nature/the work of the devil/the actions of peasants, and so he sentences them to a life in prison/to exile/to death.

As Falstaff's death is described we hear that he cried out against drink/said how much he hated the king/left a will, and the Boy also describes the way that he spoke out against children/the aristocracy/women. As Pistol is about to leave for France he advises the Hostess, his daughter/wife/grandmother, to look after his belongings/not to wander at night/to work hard.

In the king's palace at Paris/Calais/Rouen, the French king orders the invasion of England/a retreat/the defence of French towns. The Dauphin assumes that England still has an idle king/has no desire for war/will be distracted by a war with Scotland, and so he is not worried. However, the Constable reports that Henry has a huge army/has changed/is going to surrender. Exeter arrives in France and demands that the French king give up the arms/lands/weapons that belong by right to England. If the French refuse, Exeter says that there will be a bloody war/further negotiation/battle at sea. There is another message, a personal one for the Dauphin, whom King Henry personally dislikes/is plotting to murder/has challenged to a duel. The Dauphin says that he presented Henry with the drink/gold/tennis balls, intending to make a mocking statement about Henry's Christianity/youth/appearance. Exeter tells the French that the English have already landed in France/are on the Channel/will invade from the north.

Who? What? Why? When? Where? How?

1 Who has Pistol married?
2 What does Bardolph achieve as he talks to Nym and Pistol?
3 Why does the Boy want the other characters to 'come in quickly'?
4 How does the king make the conspirators think that they are safe?
5 What do Cambridge, Scroop and Gray think about Henry's proposal to 'enlarge the man committed yesterday?'
6 With which of the three conspirators is the king most angry?
7 Who talked of the Whore of Babylon – where, and why?
8 Who is described by whom as 'a vain, giddy, shallow, humourous youth'?
9 When will the French king give an answer to the English demands?
10 According to Exeter, how will the French find a difference in Henry?

Who said that, and to whom?

1 '… for the gilt of France (oh, guilt indeed)'
2 '… thou prick-eared cur of Iceland'
3 'He is so shaked to a burning quotidien tertian that it is lamentable to behold'
4 'So service shall with steelèd sinews toil'
5 'Oh, let us yet be merciful'
6 'Wouldst thou have practised on me for thy use?'
7 'My fault, but not my body, pardon, sovereign'
8 'Do you not remember 'a saw a flea…'
9 'It is most meet we arm against the foe'
10 'He'll call you to so hot an answer of it'

Explain the importance of:

1 Thriving armourers and pastures sold to buy horses.
2 Swords drawn and sheathed.
3 A heart broken by a king.
4 Papers which lead to an immediate confession.
5 'Another fall of man'.
6 'Arthur's bosom'.
7 Blood-sucking.
8 The defence of towns of war.
9 Edward, black Prince of Wales.
10 Even if there is peace, there is one character who desires 'nothing but odds'.

Act 3

The Chorus gives us two important pieces of information. The English army is embarking to set sail towards Harfleur in France, and the French king has offered his daughter to Henry in marriage, along with a dowry. Unfortunately, the dowry is a number of worthless kingdoms.

'…this fleet majestical…'

Chorus

Can you see how Chorus expresses the mood of the English nation as it is going to war? The descriptions of the embarkation and the voyage across the Channel suggest a hurried, bustling scene. Do you think this says something about the confidence and patriotism of the English?

'Grapple your minds'

This speech is a good illustration of how Shakespeare uses the lines of the

War

Chorus to present a strong visual picture of a scene that is important to the development of the play, but very hard to portray on the stage. There is a marvellous realism in lines such as: 'Upon the hempen tackle ship-boys climbing'.

In a play dealing with such huge events across two countries, the Chorus is also able to provide news of a dramatic

event which helps to progress the plot. Henry 'likes not' the offer of the hand of the French Princess in marriage with the useless dowry. Don't be confused by this: he will eventually marry her, under terms which secure peace, but does not accept this present offer as a way of preventing the war.

Act 3, scene 1

There is an attack on Harfleur. Henry drives his men on, inspiring them to advance courageously, appealing to their nobility as Englishmen and to their manhood.

'Once more unto the breach, dear friends, once more'

This is our first glimpse of the way that Henry can use language as a powerful

Rhetoric

part of his armoury at war. Look at the sorts of rhetorical devices he uses to win over the hearts of his men, to give them confidence in themselves and to lead them into battle. Analyse the speech and see if you can discover the changes in pace and the effects of the imagery, especially the extended metaphor which starts with 'stiffening sinews in the action of the tiger'.

Henry shows signs here of being a great leader. Certainly he knows how to appeal to the men. Put yourself in the position of one of the ordinary soldiers: how would you feel if you were reminded at this hour of your honourable warlike ancestors and the importance of not 'dishonouring your mother'?

The speech is like a trumpet call. It seems to rise in tone and drama throughout, and the climax at the end with the lines 'Cry "God for Harry, England and Saint George!"' is intended to stir the soul of even the meanest coward. Notice also the way that Henry speaks very directly to his men, as if he were taking a personal interest in them. This is a technique he uses again later in the play, at the Battle of Agincourt.

Act 3, scene 2

In this scene we are shown the cowardice of Bardolph, Pistol and Nym. They are positioned behind the front lines attacking Harfleur and have to be driven on by Captain Llewellyn. The Boy is disgusted by their cowardice and as they are being moved forward into battle by Llewellyn, he describes some of their behaviour since they have been in France.

'these three swashers...'

As you observe the scurrilous behaviour of Bardolph, Pistol and Nym, think about the way they openly admit their cowardice. In stark contrast to the tone of the king's speech in the previous scene, Nym declares that the 'knocks are too hot' – in other words, for him and his company of friends, the fighting is too fierce. They would rather be back at home in a London alehouse. There are interesting descriptions of each of them: Bardolph looks the part of a soldier but hangs back from fighting; Pistol says all the right things but is a man of no action; and the only violence that Nym has done to anyone is to himself when drunk. But the Boy reveals that cowardice is not their only shortcoming as soldiers: they also steal. Some of the theft they have been engaged in is described by the Boy.

'... pocketing up of wrongs'

So upset and disillusioned is the Boy that he wants to leave the three men 'and seek some better service'. There are three points worth thinking about when you read this scene. Firstly, do not forget the context in which these comic characters appear in the play: remember that they were friends of Henry in his disreputable past. Now they are behaving in the same way as all the associates of Falstaff used to, including the king himself. Can you see how their behaviour may serve to remind us of how Henry has changed?

Secondly, their cowardice and 'war crimes' (pilfering was a crime) present a rather different view of the English war effort in comparison with the words and actions of the king and the nobility. One final point to note about this scene: the audience is introduced to the Welsh captain, Llewellyn, who is going to play a major part in later events. Unlike Bardolph, Pistol and Nym, he is a very loyal soldier.

Puns

The play is rich in its language. The king's rhetoric and frequent stirring poetry are matched by other characters who are also given opportunities for varied and entertaining language. In a manner that seems to stress his innocence, the Boy here uses a series of puns to describe his dislike of the cowardice of the three 'swashers'. For example, 'it is plain pocketing up of wrongs' means that it is against the law. The phrase also describes the receiving of stolen goods. Now look at the final sentence: can you detect a rather unsavoury double meaning? Might the Boy be trying to conceal his true meanings by putting them over in such a roundabout way?

Act 3, scene 3

Llewellyn is worried about the way that the mining around Harfleur has been incompetent. He is critical of the work of the Irishman, Captain MacMorris. Llewellyn and MacMorris argue about the rules of war.

Disciplines of the war

There are perhaps three important features of this scene, although in other respects it has no real bearing on events.

Llewellyn

We are introduced in more detail here to Llewellyn, who is going to play such a loyal and important part in events later. He is seen here to be a determined character, even rather a busybody, certainly a man full of his own opinions.

We are also given some insight into the techniques of war. The way that wars were fought was changing, but Llewellyn finds this hard. He would prefer to stick to the old principles, the 'disciplines of the pristine wars of the Romans'. MacMorris, given a free hand, would have been much more direct and 'would have blowed up the town... in an hour'.

The other point worthy of consideration is the fact that these men, all from different parts of the country (notice there is an Englishman, an Irishman, a Welshman and a Scotsman, each with exaggerated characteristics of speech), are quarrelling amongst themselves. Do you gain a strong impression of national unity as the country fights with France? Both this and the preceding scene may force us to think again about how unified this war effort is, in spite of all the fine words from the king.

Act 3, scene 4

Henry speaks first to the Governor of Harfleur and then directly to the people. He persuades them to surrender, describing the consequences if they fail to give in to his advancing army. He says that he will not be able to control his soldiers if they are let loose on the town. The Governor, who has received no help from the Dauphin, agrees to surrender.

'Waste and desolation'

This is a vivid impression of the horrors of war, one of a number of speeches

War

in the play which, whether Shakespeare intended the effect or not, present war as a theme in its own right. Henry says that if there is no surrender, then he will not be responsible for leading his army in a disciplined manner any longer. He describes, with the help of some of the most violent imagery of the play, the way that his soldiers will slaughter 'your fresh fair virgins and your flowering infants'. There will be rape, violence and murder once the soldiers are beyond his command.

Henry uses language in an effective and rhetorical way, perhaps giving some foresight into how he will use speeches to his men to such great effect later, at Agincourt. He succeeds with the Governor because he paints such a horrific picture of the consequences if there is no surrender. His imagery is very strong – see how at one point he says that holding back his soldiers will be as practical as persuading the Leviathan to come ashore, and later how the 'mad mothers with their howls' would be like the: 'wives of Jewry, At Herod's bloody-hunting slaughtermen'.

'sickness growing upon our soldiers...'

Henry is certainly speaking to the Governor of Harfleur, but who else will be listening? Remember that his army is sick and weak, and, as we learn right at the end of the scene, the winter is coming on. Might he be trying to motivate his own men as well as gain the surrender of Harfleur? He says that they will only stay one night in Harfleur. Might his army have needed some encouragement to move on to Calais the next day? Would his style of speech have provided this much-needed boost to their morale?

War

Act 3, scene 5

This scene shows the French princess, Katherine, in conversation with her gentlewoman, Alice. The princess is given a lesson in some basic English words but as the lesson continues she is struck by the fact that some of the English words sound like rude French words!

'les mots... non pour les dames d'honneur d'user'

In many ways this is a scene of light relief within the intensity of the war. It is spoken in French, the princess learning 'pidgin English'. Sometimes in a play of intense action, it is important to provide the audience with some relief, but that is not the only reason for its inclusion. Katherine has already been offered as a sort of ransom to King Henry, but this offer has been turned down. However, he will of course marry her later and this will be part of the peace treaty. In the epic structure of the play it is important that Katherine is introduced and aspects of her character established. To become a complete king, Henry must marry. Katherine comes across as coy and impressionable, just as a princess should. There is a predictable modesty about her, yet you might also notice the natural human way that she appears to enjoy her discovery that the English words sound like rude French ones. Having made this shocking discovery, she wants to continue her lesson all over again!

Princess Katherine

If you read this scene in conjunction with the latter part of Act 5, scene 2, you will get an impression of how attractive this demure princess is going to be to the English king.

Act 3, scene 6

Constable and the French king are concerned to hear about the English advances. They question the worth of their own honour if they are going to stand by and allow the English to march on unchecked. They mock the English, but all the while they are aware that French women are mocking them. The French king first orders his lords to try to defeat Henry and bring him back as a prisoner to the French court, but then he has another idea: because, he thinks, the English will be so afraid of the French army at the sight of their numbers, Henry will submit himself as ransom. He orders the dispatch of Montjoy to arrange this ransom.

'that nook-shotten isle of Albion'

You will recall how the Dauphin underestimated the English when he foolishly sent the mocking gift of tennis balls to King Henry in Act 1. Here again we find that the French are living with false perceptions. Whilst they do betray their own nervousness and feelings of inadequacy about the unchecked advance of the English troops, they are foolishly contemptuous about the English. Just as they started to do so in Act 2, they mock the quaint ways of the English. To them, it is particularly laughable that English ale is like 'sodden water', of use only as 'a drench for sur-reined jades'.

'Let us not hang like roping icicles
Upon our houses' thatch whiles a more frosty people
Sweat drops of gallant youth in our rich fields'

In truth, in spite of the humour they derive from making fun of the English, they are ashamed, and they know that French women are laughing at their failure. It is an inward-looking scene, almost as if the French nobles need to reassure themselves of their superiority. Notice the complex way in which images associated with ice and frost are used, perhaps suggesting a cold fear of what is to come.

High dukes, great princes, barons, lords and knights

War

As the epic struggle develops, the French king calls upon all his noblemen, in a huge show of strength. Lines 40 to 45 show an impressive list of all the great men of France as they are called to arms. Remember that, by comparison, the English army is weak and tired and will be massively outnumbered. The French are confident that the English king will submit, and Montjoy is sent to negotiate his ransom.

Act 3, scene 7

This scene describes a crucial moment in the advance of the English army. They had to cross the River Ternoise and the bridge across it needed defending. Llewellyn describes the bravery of Exeter, and what he assumes was the bravery of Lieutenant Pistol, in their defence of the bridge. Pistol arrives and asks Llewellyn to persuade the Duke of Exeter to save the life of his old friend Bardolph, who is sentenced to death for the theft of a crucifix from a church. He fails, so Bardolph must die. Gower informs Llewellyn that Pistol is just a braggart, a man of brave words, but really a coward. Llewellyn reports Bardolph's crime to the king, who orders his death. Montjoy arrives and asks Henry to consider what he might offer as ransom. Henry sends back a clear message: there will be no ransom. He will march on and fight to the bitter end. He orders his men to march on to the river and set up camp for the night.

A lot happens in this scene. It brings together a number of features and key themes in the play. Ask yourself the question: what has changed by the end of the scene?

'an anchient lieutenant there at the pridge'

Pistol is exposed. The scene starts with Llewellyn praising his bravery in

helping Exeter defend the bridge at Ternoise. What has Llewellyn been taken in by? At one point he says of Pistol: 'he is as valiant a man as Mark Antony'! Later, Gower puts him right. Pistol is that breed of soldier who knows how to look the part in every respect. They know all the names of the great commanders, they can reel off by heart where all the

Tavern characters

battles have been fought. They return home with the same cut of beard as their general and also appear authentic by the bloodstains on their battle coats. In reality, however, they are dreadful cowards. Where else do we come across Pistol's cowardice and his clever way with words?

Bardolph

How we should react to Bardolph's death is open to interpretation. Pistol shows his own style of morality as he tries to intervene on behalf of his old friend. Equally, as we come to know Llewellyn as a character, it does not surprise us that he should stand firm and preach about the need for execution: 'if, look you, he were my brother I would desire the duke to use his good pleasure and put him to execution. Poor discipline ought to be used'.

'We shall have all such offenders so cut off'

It is perhaps the king's reaction that we are most interested in here. Without knowledge of *Henry IV, Parts i and ii*, it is difficult to realise the full significance of this hanging. Bardolph was one of Prince Hal's greatest chums when he frequented 'The Boar's Head' tavern in his youth. There was even one

Henry V

occasion, near the start of *Henry IV, Part i*, when Prince Hal played a trick on his friends, including Bardolph, knowing that they were involved in a robbery.

So what do we make of this decision to hang Bardolph? Is it a sign that King Henry has finally reformed and that his foolish past is now buried forever? If so, how do we interpret his practical joke later to be played at Llewellyn's expense? Does he feel guilt at condemning his old friend to death? Is it an opportunity for a show of authority? Should he have shown leniency, as Pistol asks, or did he simply have no choice? However we view the event, it does seem that Henry's reformation is finally complete. This is his second show of ruthless authority.

'Thus says my king...'

French court

Montjoy's speech is further proof that the French are misjudging events. As he speaks, he exaggerates the French position of strength and the English weaknesses. He claims that they could have won at Harfleur, 'but that we thought not good to bruise an injury till it were full ripe'. He tells the English that they will regret their foolishness and come to suffer from their own weakness. He sets out his terms for a ransom, and with each term insults the English king.

'Yet forgive me, God, that I do brag thus'

Henry V

Henry is not put off by Montjoy's language. He describes the weakness of his army, but insults the French by stating how, when fit, each man was worth three Frenchmen. His only offer of ransom is his body. The English will march on. If they are not allowed free passage, they will fight to the end. He serves warning on the French in uncompromising language : 'If we be hindered, we shall your tawny ground with your red blood discolour'.

'We are in God's hand, brother, not in theirs'

Religion

The scene ends on a familiar theme, Henry drawing strength from religion. This is definitely a Christian war, with right on the side of the English king. Think about how such a view would have been received by a patriotic Elizabethan audience. The omens are not good for the English at this point. They are badly outnumbered and weakened, yet they march on with a determined leader and God on their side.

Act 3, scene 8

It is the night before the Battle of Agincourt. The French nobles are assembled, and spend their time bragging amongst each other about their horses and making sexual puns. Bourbon leaves to prepare for the battle and the Constable and Orleans talk about him behind his back. As they do so, this leads them into another conversation, about proverbs. A messenger arrives to tell them that the English army is close by. They mock the English again.

A long night

You can break this scene down into sections. Firstly, there are the boasts about

the horses, Bourbon's being perhaps the most colourful and far-fetched. Then look at the way that this turns into the puns about Bourbon's mistress (the rudest is the double meaning in lines 52–53: 'They that ride so and ride not warily fall into foul bogs' means, amongst other things, catching a foul sexual disease from parts of a woman's body). Note also that a 'jade' is both an old horse and a whore! Ask yourself why these men are spending their time, the night before a major battle, holding such a frivolous conversation. The third section is the battle of proverbs between Orleans and the Constable. Again, it is a seemingly pointless conversation.

Orleans: 'It is now two o'clock.'

Both sides are nervous. In Act 4, scene 1, we are about to discover Henry himself roving the English camp by night and some of his soldiers voicing their fears of the coming battle.

Similarly, during their impatient night of waiting for battle, near Agincourt, the French camp is tense. Distracted, nervous, their aimless bragging turns to smut and then to further bragging as they try to outsmart each other with clever proverbs. You might also feel that Orleans and the Constable are being sarcastic towards Bourbon, and that their tone continues to mock him behind his back.

How do these petty arguments reveal the mood of the French nobles? Are they quite as confident as they suggest near the end of the scene after hearing of the closeness of the English camp? Consider also the animal imagery used by them about the English near the end of the scene. How might this imagery show their *over*-confidence?

Self-test Questions Act 3

Uncover the plot
Delete two of the three alternatives given, to find the correct plot. Beware possible misconceptions and muddles.

Chorus describes the departure of the English troops for Calais/Rouen/Harfleur and explains that a treaty is proposed by the French involving the offer of marriage to Princess Katherine/the lands of Burgundy/joint rule of France. The king persuades his troops to fight in the siege of Harfleur by imitating a storm/tiger/cannon, but this has little effect on Pistol and Nym, who spend their time singing/gambling/sleeping instead of going forward. The Boy is delighted by their cleverness/upset by their language/disgusted by their cowardice. Llewellyn and MacMorris discuss the tactics for entering the town/the mining/the morale of the soldiers. After the siege, the king demands that the governor pays a ransom/submits/hands over his weapons. If there is no agreement, Henry says that he will not be responsible for his soldiers' actions/his own temper/the upkeep of the town.

Whilst learning some English words, Princess Katherine discovers that she is a quick learner/that her gentlewoman has no patience/that some of the words sound rude. The French nobles are surprised at the English advances and insult England. They think of the English climate as mild/damp/bright and the ale as bitter/sweet/weak. The Constable is sure that, when he sees the French army/Dauphin/nobles, King Henry will want to offer a ransom/turn back/fight to the end.

Whilst defending/mending/destroying the bridge at Ternoise, Pistol convinces Llewellyn that he is strong/good with words/a brave soldier, but Llewellyn is later told the truth by the king/Gower/Exeter. Bardolph is sentenced to hang because he has stolen a crucifix/killed a woman/behaved like a coward. Montjoy arrives to negotiate a ransom/offer the English a treaty/rebuke the king, but Henry stands firm. During the night before the battle, Bourbon brags about his armour/horse/weapons before he and other French nobles start to think about the future/plan tactics/make rude jokes. The French noblemen mock the English and compare their soldiers to dogs/snakes/insects.

Who? What? Why? When? Where? How?

1   What are offered to the king which are worthless?
2   At Harfleur, who does Henry tell the English troops not to dishonour?
3   Why does the Boy feel disappointed with Pistol, Nym and Bardolph?
4   Who refuses to discuss theory when more action is required?
5   If the gates of Harfleur are not opened, what will happen to Henry's troops?
6   When Katherine is learning English, what does she discover about the language?
7   How is Llewellyn deceived about Pistol?
8   Where does Henry want to march on to 'without impeachment'?
9   What answer does Henry give Montjoy?
10 Why do the French nobles find the conversation about horses funny?

Who said that, and to whom?

1   'Now set the teeth and stretch the nostril wide'
2   'Cry "God for Harry, England and Saint George!"'
3   'The knocks are too hot, and for mine own part I have not a case of lives'
4   'It is no time to discourse… the town is beseeched!'
5   'We yield our town and lives to thy soft mercy'
6   'Our madams mock at us'
7   'Fortune is painted plind'
8   'We would have all such offenders so cut off'
9   'You are as well provided of both as any prince in the world'
10 'Foolish curs, that run winking into the mouth of a Russian bear'

Explain the importance of:

1   A daughter.
2   'Greyhounds in the slips.'

3   A soldier who is 'white-livered' and 'red-faced'.
4   Conclavities which are insufficient.
5   The Leviathan.
6   Parts of the body.
7   Dances.
8   A pax.
9   The Duke of Exeter's success.
10 The air of France.

Act 4

Chorus describes the preparations for war in the two camps on the night before the Battle of Agincourt. The French are confident; they play at dice. The outnumbered English are thinking about the likely disaster that awaits them. Chorus also describes the way that King Henry walks amongst his soldiers to raise their spirits.

'The confident and over-lusty French... the poor condemnèd English'

Chorus contrasts the mood of the two camps. The French are over-confident

Chorus

– not surprisingly, as they are much stronger than the English. So certain are they of victory, they play a dice game, gambling with the 'low-rated English'.

Throughout his speech, Chorus personifies night, but the French are not scared by its presence. They 'chide the cripple tardy-gaited night' (slow moving darkness), and so she (night) 'doth limp so tediously away... like a foul and ugly witch'.

Chorus sets up the conditions for the epic struggle which is about to take place: a fight between an army of great strength and the courageous but nervous underdogs.

Act 4, scene 1

Henry tells Gloucester that they must turn their weakness into a positive advantage. He borrows Erpingham's cloak in order to go amongst his men in disguise. In an important part of the play, various things happen to Henry whilst he is in disguise. Firstly he is challenged by Pistol, who does not recognise him. Then Llewellyn appears and demands quiet in the camp, even though the French are making a lot of noise.

The king stumbles across three soldiers, Court, Williams and Bates, and has a conversation with them about the war. Williams and Bates hold the view that the king is responsible for the salvation or damnation of soldiers who die in battle. Henry puts over a different view; that each individual is responsible for the state of his own soul before death. This leads to an argument. Williams believes that the king will be ransomed when he wants to be. A challenge is declared: Williams and the king (in disguise) exchange gloves and Williams says that if he sees the king again, he will strike him. The scene ends with the king thinking to himself about the burden of kingship, and about the trappings of ceremony that come with being the monarch.

'There is some soul of goodness in things evil'

On of the finest qualities of Henry's leadership is his ability to affect the

Henry V

morale of his troops when they are at their lowest ebb. He reveals that this will be his tactic. He contrasts the danger they are in with the courage they will need: ''tis true that we are in great danger. The greater therefore should our courage be'.

This stirring style of leadership is brought out in later scenes when he needs to motivate his men in the battle. We also see, in the first speech of the act, that he is going to use language in a highly poetic and rhetorical way in order to be persuasive amongst the English army. One of his great weapons at war will be his language: for example, he says: 'Thus may we gather honey from the weed and make a moral of the devil himself'.

Think about the fact that Henry is speaking in these poetic terms as he approaches the battle. Do you find that he is consciously using language in a particular way? What might he intend with such a style of speech? Why is it so important that he should persuade his men to make light of their burdens?

'Lend me thy cloak, Sir Thomas'

Henry borrows Sir Thomas' cloak in order to move disguised amongst his

Conspiracy

men in the camp. In spite of his earlier brave words to Gloucester, this scene reveals some of his anxieties. It is an important part of the play, perhaps arguably its centre, or core, and the symbol of disguise is important, raising as it does the question: who is the real king? The key theme of the nature of kingship is explored through the mediations which take

place in the king's conversations with some of his men in disguise.

'My name is Pistol called'

The brief meeting between the king and Pistol seems to confirm that Henry cannot be recognised. They would have known each other from their days in 'The Boar's Head' tavern. Pistol begins with a nostalgic memory of the king, and praises him. He recalls him affectionately as 'a lad of life, an imp of fame', but later insults this man, in disguise, after the king reveals that he is a friend of Llewellyn's. In a sense, Pistol is being mocked. He praises the king with one breath, and then – without realising it – insults him with the next!

'no tiddle taddle nor pibble pabble...'

A sort of sub-plot is developing based on the animosity, or dislike, that exists

Llewellyn

between Pistol and Llewellyn. Remember the reasons for this, especially the way that Llewellyn treated Pistol's old friend Bardolph. Llewellyn continues here in the same mould of behaviour. Righteously insisting on discipline in the English camp, he demands that there should be less noise, even though there is a lot of noise coming from the French. This fits into his desire for orderly and proper behaviour, and gains praise from the king himself.

'the king is but a man as I am'

The conversation between the king and the two soldiers, Williams and Bates,

Rhetoric

all takes place in prose. Henry has forsaken the eloquence of noble poetry as he here talks openly to ordinary men about his innermost thoughts. The rhetoric has gone as he searches for honest speech to say what he really means. From the things he says, we learn a great deal about the nature of kingship. It is as though, having stepped outside his real self

through the disguise, Henry can contemplate the burdens of his role as monarch. He makes a number of observations and arguments, and Bates and Williams have a number of points to make to him.

'in his nakedness he appears but a man'

A king is equally, in reality, a mere man. His fears are the same as those of ordinary men, but he needs to mask them or he will have an adverse effect on the morale of his men.

'If his cause be wrong...'

Bates and Williams lead the conversation around to a consideration of the way

Henry V

that the king has a responsibility for the salvation of his soldiers. They say they will have to die dismal deaths in battle without the opportunity of salvation or redemption.

Williams says: 'I am afeard there are few die well that die in a battle, for how can they charitably dispose of anything when blood is their argument?' For a soldier to 'die well', as

Williams says, or to 'charitably dispose of anything', he would need to die with his soul in an acceptable state for God – a state of goodness, of love and redemption from sins on earth. But this is not easy in battle, where men are required to kill. There is another twist to his argument: men are required to kill for the king, and the king, according to divine medieval law, is God's deputy on earth. So the soldier is trapped, argues Williams: he has to fight, to obey the king; he perhaps has to die, but he cannot die with his sins absolved, and without salvation, he will go to Hell. This is why the king bears such a strong responsibility.

'all those legs and arms and heads, chopped off in a battle'

Williams shows how strongly he feels through his vivid description of death in battle between lines 123 and 129. Can you see what he might be thinking about here? Does he have a vision of what might happen in the coming battle? Notice also the way that one of these characters, Bates, says only one thing at the start of this conversation. What is going through *his* mind as he sits and listens to the rest of what is said?

War

'every subject's soul is his own'

Henry replies that a king cannot be responsible for the earlier sins of his subjects, any more than can the father for his son's or the master for his servant's. Soldiers, he argues, take with them into battle all the guilt of their past crimes and 'though they can outstrip men they have no wings to fly from God'. The soldier should welcome death as an advantage once he has washed 'every mote out of his conscience', and if he escapes death, this is God's way of letting him teach others of God's goodness that he has witnessed in his confession.

Henry V

'... when our throats are cut he may be ransomed and we ne'er the wiser'

Following the conversation about the salvation of the soldier, they turn to the issue of ransom, and Williams shows a gulf between the thinking of ordinary people and the king. Williams, cynically, does not believe that the king will not be ransomed. He is saying that all King Henry has to do is wait until they are dead and then ransom himself in order to avoid death himself. Like many of the characters in the play, Williams shows that he has a clever way with words as he makes his points with two interesting images. Henry says that, if the king is ransomed, he will never trust him again. Williams likens this to 'a perilous shot out of an elder gun', meaning that for an ordinary person to talk about trusting the king is like trying to threaten somebody with a toy gun (ie one made out of elder wood) – in other words, an irrelevant thing to say! With considerable wit he also says, as if speaking a wise proverb: 'You may as well go about to turn the sun to ice with fanning in his face with a peacock's feather'.

Both Williams and the king are angry, but they have no time to pursue their quarrel now, and so exchange gloves in order to recognise each other later. Williams threatens that when he finds his enemy 'I will take thee a box on the ear'. Henry is going to make use of this quarrel later. Why has he 'embraced' it? What has annoyed him so much? Were there, after all, dangers in roaming amongst his men in disguise?

'What infinite heart's ease must kings neglect That private men enjoy?'

In what is by far the most reflective moment in the play, Henry, left to himself, speaks a soliloquy. The theme of kingship has been evident in many forms. We have seen the king as a reformed character, capable of ruthless decisions. He is a man of religion. He has authority, a sense of justice and can plan well. He is heroic in battle and a strong leader, never shirking responsibility. He is a truly epic hero, the ideal Christian king. But now we are led inside his mind, and we find that it is troubled.

Rhetoric

'idol ceremony'

What, he asks, does a king possess that ordinary men do not have, save 'ceremony'? He personifies ceremony. As if it were a god, he asks: what are you except for 'place, degree and form,/Creating awe and fear in other men?' He becomes agitated with the weaknesses and inadequacies of ceremony, 'thou proud dream,/That playst so subtly with a king's repose'.

'the wretched slave'

In the second half of the soliloquy, Henry thinks about the life of the lowly

slave or peasant, who sleeps soundly after an honest day's work, unaware of what the king is doing to 'maintain the peace'. The feelings here are a mixture of anguish and envy. The king, with all his powers and responsibilities, must lead his men into battle and forget that he is an ordinary person, and yet he can live with none of the peace of mind that

Henry V

belongs to the slave or peasant. Notice how a wonderful moment of alliteration brings out these bitter feelings: '(The slave)… in gross brain little wots what watch the king keeps to maintain the peace'.

Act 4, scene 2

As the sun comes up, the French are eager to fight. They think that because of their superior numbers, the English will easily be defeated. They are encouraged by Grandpré's description of the haggard English army.

'Why do you stay so long, my Lords of France? Yon island carrions, desperate of their bones, Ill favouredly become the morning field'

At the start of the play, remember how Chorus asked the audience to use its

War

imagination on a grand scale because of the events taking place. In this part of the play, as battle approaches, we move from camp to camp, and get impressions of the preparations of both the English and the French. The epic structure of the play requires that we need to know just how strong the French are and how weak the English army is. The language of the French is enthusiastic: they are ready for the battle. The Constable declares that even the horses are keen to start: 'Hark how our steeds for present service neigh'. Grandpré describes the English banners in a contemptuous and insulting phrase: 'Their ragged curtains poorly are let loose/And our air shakes them passing scornfully'.

'A very little little let us do, and all is done'

French court

Shakespeare also reveals the complacency of the French through the way they speak so lightly about their task. They even joke about sending the English 'dinners and fresh suits' to feed them up and make them look more like an army. These lines need to be contrasted with their despair in Act 4, scene 5, when their ranks have been surprisingly broken by the plucky English and they are facing 'everlasting shame'.

However, as the story of the epic struggle develops, the audience may well be feeling worried here about the English. The battle appears to be a lost cause for them; they seem to have no hope.

Act 4, scene 3

The English lords try to remain brave and calm, despite being so heavily outnumbered. Westmorland laments the fact that there are not more men in the field. The king turns this despair to his advantage and stirs his men into battle with a speech in which he encourages them to become a 'band of brothers'. The English go forward into position for battle. Montjoy comes over from the French side and once more asks Henry to name his ransom. Henry bitterly refuses and commands his men into battle.

'five to one... all are fresh'

War

Shakespeare is about to tell of one of the most remarkable events in history. The French outnumber the English five to one, and the English lords are despondent, although Bedford and Exeter try to put a brave face on events, wishing each other good fortune. Westmorland is even more despondent, and his words provoke the king to utter his most powerful speech: 'O that we now had here but one ten thousand of those men in England that do no work today'.

'We few, we happy few, we band of brothers - For he today that sheds his blood with me Shall be my brother'

Rhetoric

The speech that follows Westmorland's doubts is unquestionably one of Shakespeare's great speeches. Henry is seen at his most persuasive, using the opportunity to turn a weak and bedraggled army into a courageous fighting unit who win a most unlikely battle through their bravery. In memorable language, the speech makes explicit the patriotic themes of honour and courage. You cannot study this play without a thorough knowledge of the speech, but as well as knowing it, you should enjoy it, for its power and emotions are gripping and it is hard not to be moved by the words. Read it aloud, for it is really one of those moments in literature which make us want to get up and take part in the action, and consequently it is easy to see why the army responds so readily.

In a carefully constructed argument, the king appeals first of all to the pride of his men. They will take possession, he says, of 'the greater share of honour' by fighting as a small army. He places 'honour' in the centre of their minds and makes them feel that they are better off fighting as they are: 'O, do not wish one more!' In fact, he says, we would not wish to die in the company of any man who was not prepared to die in 'fellowship... with us'.

Henry makes great play of the fact that this day is the eve of a saint's day: the Feast of Crispian. He builds up his rhetoric in this part of the speech to persuade his men into thinking that this will truly be a wonderful day on which to fight. He appeals to their emotions by telling them how proud they can be in the future to be able to say that 'These wounds I had on Crispin's day'.

Another ploy Henry uses is to persuade his men into thinking that they are in a brotherhood with himself and the other nobles. In a passage full of alliteration, spoken with the passion of a preacher, he appeals to the men as if he knew and loved them personally (look at lines 60–67). Can you see the effects of the alliteration? Incidentally, it is a speech on which politicians and world leaders in the twentieth century have based their ideas and drawn inspiration for stirring language. Can you see why this might have been the case?

'Thou dost not wish more help from England, coz?'

War

Henry's language has done the trick. Salisbury encourages Henry to move urgently into position for the battle to begin and Westmorland is now full of courage: 'God's will, my liege, would you and I alone, without more help, could fight this royal battle'.

'... thou art so near the gulf
Thou needs must be englutted'

Henry is of course in no mood to offer himself as ransom. 'Achieve me,' he says 'and then sell my bones'! He knows his men are listening, and so he continues in the same vein as in the 'band of brothers' speech. Yes, Englishmen will die, he agrees, but they will die valiantly. In any event, their 'earthly parts' will 'choke your clime' and 'the smell whereof shall breed a plague in France'. This, he says, will kill more Frenchmen, so the English will continue to show their valour even when they are dead. Speak no more of ransom, he tells the herald, Montjoy: we may look weak, but our 'hearts are in the trim'. He makes the English think for the first time that they can actually win the battle, and in doing so he insults the French: 'they' (the English army) 'will pluck the gay new coats o'er the French soldiers' heads and turn them out of service'. At the end of the scene, why does Henry say: 'I fear thou wilt once more come again for a ransom', and why does York want to lead the vanguard (the troops at the front)?

Act 4, scene 4

Pistol takes a French lord as prisoner, but through the translations of the Boy, he accepts a ransom. The Boy is so disgusted at Pistol's cowardice, he says that even Bardolph and Nym were braver.

'As I suck blood...'

When Pistol takes the French lord as his prisoner, his only interest is in

gaining money. This is a return to the 'blood sucking' of the sub-plot. Pistol shows no guts. He gets the Boy to translate for him in order to secure a ransom. The Boy is now so disgusted with Pistol's cowardice, he even recalls Bardolph and Nym as being ten times more brave! The Boy gives us further insight into the character of Pistol by commenting on the way that he has a lot to say for himself: 'the empty vessel makes the greatest sound'.

Valour

Notice that once again, the play's structure depends on contrasts. Honour is undermined by the placing of a scene such as this, about cowardice, following after the more noble passages of the play.

Act 4, scene 5

The French are facing defeat. Their ranks are broken, and they admit eternal shame. Bourbon is prepared for another attack, wishing to die honourably rather than die in the shame of defeat.

This is a very short scene, all about the feelings of defeat. In a very short period of time within this epic struggle, the French are facing ignominious defeat. The description of their shame is expressed in despairing language, and because of their shame they are prepared to face death: 'The devil take order now, I'll to the throng. Let life be short, else shame will be too long'.

Act 4, scene 6

Exeter describes, in emotional detail, the death of the Duke of York. Henry is moved by what he hears concerning York's death, and forgives Exeter his tears. He orders that all French prisoners should be executed.

Tears

Notice the techniques that Exeter uses in his language to describe the noble deaths of Suffolk and York. It is a touching description, reinforcing the themes of patriotism, heroism and chivalry. The king is moved, but he makes a curious decision: he orders the killing of all French prisoners. Although there was no convention for behaviour in war, as there is today (the Geneva Convention), the laws of chivalry did not permit the killing of prisoners. Henry shows a possible weakness in his character as he breaks the code of combat by wrongfully ordering the deaths of the prisoners. There is an added poignancy to his behaviour as the next scene also describes a type of 'war crime'.

Act 4, scene 7

The French have killed the luggage boys, strictly 'against the law of arms', as Llewellyn points out. The king is also incensed at the killing of the boys, and reaffirms that he wants the throats of all the prisoners cut. Montjoy arrives to claim the Frenchmen who have died. The French admit defeat and Henry names the battle 'Agincourt' after a nearby castle. Llewllyn discourses with the king about his Welsh ancestry. Henry wants to know how many men have died. He also asks Williams about the glove that is worn in his hat and asks Llewellyn's advice about the challenge. By giving Llewellyn Williams' glove, he sets up a fight between Llewellyn and Williams, but then thinks twice about the possible consequences and sends his lords to prevent the fight taking place!

'Kill the poys and the luggage! 'Tis expressly against the laws of arms'

Llewellyn

Another wrongful act, the killing of the luggage boys, moves both Llewellyn and the king. Why do you think Llewelyn becomes distracted, talking about the king's greatness at such an important moment in the play? Their conversation, over the bodies of the luggage boys, is almost humorous. They debate a point about the king's greatness, with Llewellyn rather absurdly drawing comparisons between the River Wye and the river at Macedon, where he is thinking about the life of Alexander the Great. Does this diversion relieve the tension? Is it intended as a comment on Llewellyn's over-eager character, that he can transfer his thoughts from one passion to another so quickly?

'I was not angry since I came to France, until this instant'

What does the king's reaction to the murders tell us about his attitude? His

Henry V

views are more directly put across than Llewellyn's, which are rather elaborate by comparison. Is this then a glimpse of the real character of the king, one who can become angry at injustice? Or is it another opportunity for him to say what is expected of him? What do you think — is it noble or opportune? Notice that Henry appears to fight fire with fire

and commits another war crime to compound the one he has been railing against: 'Besides, we'll cut the throats of these we have, and not a man of them that we shall take shall taste our mercy'.

Is it acceptable that the king should have the prisoners killed? Does this suggest a natural emotional side to a great leader for whose anger we must have understanding, or should Henry better control his feelings and act in a more dignified manner?

Exeter: 'Here comes the herald of the French, my liege'
Gloucester: 'His eyes are humbler than they used to be'

The English have won, and Montjoy's speech is spoken with a fitting humility

French court

which we have not yet heard from the French. They now not only accept that they have lost the battle, but they do so with grace and there is a complete change in their outlook. King Henry is honoured by Montjoy: 'Oh, give us leave, great king, to view the field in safety, and dispose of their dead bodies'.

Look carefully at the other things he says in his speech

beginning on line 60. It is a terrifying impression of the defeat that the French have suffered. What does his language tell us about the valour of the English?

'I know not if the day be ours or no'

How do you interpret the king's reaction to the victory? Is he genuinely saying

Henry V

here that he does not know if the battle is won? If so, it may suggest that he has been so personally involved in the fighting that he is unaware of what has happened. His words may suggest that he has genuinely been fighting in a form of brotherhood with his men.

Henry proudly names the battle 'Agincourt' and reminds

his men that it has been nobly fought on the 'day of Crispin Crispianus'.

'A most prave pattle...'

There are some interesting twists to the events at this point, which in many ways is the climax of the play. Llewellyn, delighted by the victory, chooses the moment to praise the king and compare him with the Black Prince. He takes great pride in Henry's Welsh ancestry. In Llewellyn's excessive reverence, we see the loyalty and gratitude of one of the king's supporters, reflecting his men's feelings. Shakespeare also establishes the idea of Llewelyn's obsession with his own Welsh nationality, which is going to play an important part in the later dispute with Pistol.

Llewellyn

Williams' glove

Following the business about Llewellyn's Welshness, there is another curious twist to the plot. At the supreme moment of victory, Henry's mood seems to lighten, and he is reminded of the incident the previous night when he (in disguise) and Williams swopped gloves and challenged each other to a duel if they encountered one another again. Henry decides to play a practical joke, involving not just Williams, but also Llewellyn. He gives Llewellyn the glove, saying that he took it in battle from a French lord. He then asks Llewellyn for advice and, predictably, Llewellyn says that if anyone challenges him whilst he is wearing the glove in his hat, then this man would be a traitor. (Henry has planted that idea in Llewellyn's mind by suggesting that a challenger would be a supporter of the French lord.)

Conspiracy

Llewelyn has over-reacted and Henry is having some fun at his expense, although he does try to stop the fight from taking place. He senses that Llewellyn will be too earnest, so he sends Warwick and Gloucester to prevent them coming to blows.

What does the joke tell us about the king? Is it a reminder in his character of his past life? He played many a joke as the young Prince Hal in his days at the tavern. At the height of his power, when victory is secure, does his true personality surface? Is it a reduction of tension after the strains of the battle? Should we judge him better for preventing the fight rather than for setting it in motion? However you consider it, it is a curious incident at such a heroic time.

Act 4, scene 8

Williams strikes Llewellyn, who is wearing the glove. Llewellyn claims that Williams is a traitor. Warwick, Gloucester, the king and Exeter arrive on the scene and the fight is prevented. The king admits to Williams that it was he who, in disguise, gave him the glove. Williams apologises for having quarrelled with the king, but Henry orders the glove to be filled with crowns and Llewelyn adds a shilling of his own.

A roll call of the dead is heard: the French have lost 10,000 men, but the English have lost only 4 men of note, and 25 others. Hymns of praise are sung in commemoration of a great victory.

''Twas I indeed thou promisèd to strike'

Henry V

Having seen him deceive Williams and Llewellyn, the audience is keen to know what the king will do to make amends. Williams has been placed in a very embarrassing position. He understands now that he was forced to quarrel with the king and he kneels in humble pardon, realising what he has done. There are a number of ideas that might occur to you about this incident. Certainly, this is behaviour reminiscent of what Henry did as a young prince. He has positively appeared to enjoy a small scheme designed to tease others, which is hardly the sort of thing we would expect of a noble king. Place yourself in Williams' situation. He would know how ruthless Henry has been with punishments for all offenders and must clearly be scared for his life, even though he explains that he did not recognise the king in his disguise. Llewellyn, loyal to every word uttered by the king, wants Williams hung. Later, however, when the king shows compassion, and rewards rather than punishes Williams, Llewellyn gets in on the act himself, handing over a shilling with a moral message attached to it, warning Williams to stay out of further brawls.

'Give him the crowns'

Is this a chance for Henry to show what a compassionate man he is, as part of the self-image of the ideal king, full of compassion for ordinary people as well as nobility? Where else have you come across Henry in such a frame of mind?

'Was ever known so great and little loss
On one part and on th'other? Take it, God,
For it is none but thine'

War

Following the names of the dead and the account of casualties on both sides, there are some concluding words about this remarkable battle. The heroic and spiritual themes of leadership and war are brought together in the triumphs. The king stresses, in moving language, that this has been a war fought with the 'arm' of God. The justness and greatness of the victory are all in the hands of God, reminding the audience of the truly epic nature of the struggle. The company leaves Agincourt to return to Calais, and then to England, singing hymns of praise.

Self-test Questions Act 4

Uncover the plot

Delete two of the three alternatives given, to find the correct plot. Beware possible misconceptions and muddles.

Chorus describes the two armies during the night/hour/week before the battle. The French play at ball games/pray/play at dice to pass the time, whilst the English sit and wait excitedly/patiently/jovially. Henry borrows a sword/horse/cloak from the Duke of Gloucester/Pistol/Sir Thomas Erpingham and goes amongst his men. He first meets Llewellyn/Pistol/Williams, who says that the king is a good man/rogue/hypocrite. Henry thinks about the problems of kingship and talks about the trappings of ceremony/the wearing of a crown/the advantages of living in a palace. He envies the peasants/women/soldiers, who do not have the burden of kingship to face up to.

As the French prepare for battle, they think of the English as a strong force/easy prey/true friends and offer to send for a ransom/hold back in the battle/send them dinners. In answer to Westmorland's/Gloucester's/Llewellyn's anxieties, the king encourages his troops to go into battle by telling them that they are lucky to be part of his brotherhood/going to be paid extra/about to receive new weapons. When Montjoy arrives for one final demand of a truce/submission/ransom, Henry tells him that he will fight to the end/think about the offer/see him again tomorrow. Pistol does take a ransom of two hundred crowns/ten shillings/a promissory note, from his French prisoner. After the victory, Henry is made angry by the numbers of the dead/the waste of the local land/the murder of the luggage boys, and in retaliation he orders the capture of all the French nobles/the destruction of the cavalry/the death of all prisoners.

Earlier, before the battle, the king has given Williams his emblem/glove/hat and looks forward to meeting him again to finish an argument/a discussion/a meal. After the battle he fools Llewellyn into thinking that Williams is a traitor, but prevents any further conflict and gives Williams money/flowers/a title.

Who? What? Why? When? Where? How?

1   Whose cloak does Henry wear for disguise?
2   From which part of the country does Pistol think the king comes?
3   Why does Llewellyn get cross with the English troops during the night?
4   According to Williams, how do men die in battle?
5   How many men has Henry got in his 'yearly pay'?
6   What does Henry notice about the date of the Battle of Agincourt?
7   What does Henry intend to offer as the only ransom?
8   With whom does the Boy compare Pistol?
9   What is Williams given in order to be recognised?
10 What are sung at the end of the battle?

Who said that, and to whom?

1   'The country cocks do crow, the clocks do toll'
2   'A little touch of Harry in the night'
3   'War is His beadle, war is His vengeance'
4   '… but when our throats are cut he may be ransomed and we ne'er the wiser'
5   'A very little little let us do,
     And all is done'
6   'We few, we happy few, we band of brothers…'
7   'As I suck blood, I will some mercy show'

8   "'Tis as arrant a piece of knavery...'
9   'For I am Welsh you know, good countryman'
10 'I will none of your money'

Explain the importance of:
1   The *fico*.
2   An exchange of gloves.
3   Ceremony.
4   Candlesticks.
5   A story taught by men to their sons.
6   An empty vessel.
7   Shame.
8   The Wye.
9   Alençon.
10 Ten thousand slain.

Act 5
Act 5, scene 1

Chorus once again apologises to the audience and begs them to accept that the events cannot be presented realistically. He describes Henry's triumphant return home and in particular, the march into London. He then describes several years of negotiation before a return to France, now for a peace treaty.

'free from vainness and self-glorious pride'

The victorious return home is described in a way that gives the audience further insight into Henry's character. He lacks any vanity in his victory celebrations and forbids himself all shows of pride. Nevertheless, it is impossible to avoid the note of triumph in the description of the entry into London, at which point he is even compared to the greatest of all generals, Julius Caesar. Henry is truly loved by all the people, as was Caesar.

Chorus

'How many would the peaceful city quit
To welcome him?'

At this point in the play, Chorus makes a contemporary reference. He is talking about the Earl of Essex in Ireland, and we gain some insight into why Shakespeare's choice of subject for his epic was so appropriate. He appeals directly to the mood of patriotism in the country at the time the play was written, and then, just as he had begged the audience to do at the start of the play, asks them to cast their imaginations over a long timespan before Henry returns to France for the negotiation of a treaty. Once again this should help you to understand the way the epic structure of the play is working: these are events which could never be condensed into a concentrated and unified time span.

Act 5, scene 2

Llewellyn has insulted Pistol, particularly about his Welshness. Now Llewellyn gets his own back by beating Pistol and forcing him to eat raw leek. He also insults him by giving him a few pence (groats) as a way of helping him overcome his injuries. Gower tells Pistol that he should not have insulted the Welshman. Pistol laments the twists of fortune and looks forward to his return to England.

'Does fortune play the hussy with me now?'

Does this scene express a triumph of of Llewellyn's virtuous behaviour over

Llewellyn

Pistol's dishonesty and cowardice? Do we end up feeling more critical of Llewellyn for his over-earnest and vindictive behaviour? He is actually very cruel towards Pistol, both beating him into submission and forcing him to eat a raw leek. Can you imagine how distasteful such an experience might have been?

Or is there something more subtle happening in the events of this scene, which is the last we see of Pistol? One interpretation that might be possible is that this is a final humiliation for Prince Hal's old associates. Bardolph and Nym have been hanged, Falstaff is dead and we now also learn that Doll Tearsheet (Shakespeare may have made a mistake and meant 'Nell') is also dead. Yet we cannot help a feeling of affection when Pistol finishes with his pun: 'to England will I steal, and there I'll steal'.

Act 5, scene 3

The kings of France and England meet at Troyes to bring about an agreement for peace. Burgundy is present as a mediator. He makes a passionate plea for peace, in a long and important speech which contrasts fertility with devastation, but Henry insists that peace is possible only if the French agree to what he wants. His main demand has changed now from earlier in the play. He is saying that he will take Katherine as his wife and then he can become heir to the throne. Various lords from both sides withdraw to negotiate and Henry stays with the Princess Katherine to woo her. He tells her that he is a simple, rough soldier and has none of the attributes associated with the great lovers and courtiers of his day. After considerable teasing, he asks her if she will marry him. He shocks her by trying to kiss her, first on the hand and then on the lips. When the lords return, Burgundy is interested in how Henry has got on with Katherine, and as they discuss her modesty, he reduces the tone of the conversation to the level of sexual innuendo. When Henry returns to the affairs of state, he finds that the king of France has agreed to his demands; the marriage with Katherine is arranged and they look forward to lasting peace between the two kingdoms.

'The venom of such looks we fairly hope Have lost their quality'

Sometimes, friendly, warm-hearted and complimentary language can really be tense and nervous. There is a kind of polite skirmishing in the opening greetings in this scene – the cordial and dignified manner of the welcomes may mask an underlying suspicion between the French and the English. Both sides are wary of each other, and it takes a powerful speech by the Duke of Burgundy to move the two parties to a point where they have the will for peace.

French court

Burgundy's speech

Throughout the play there have been some powerful and heroic ideas spoken about war. Now it is the turn of peace to take centre stage. Burgundy uses complex poetic techniques to achieve contrasts between the terrible waste of war and the fertility and creative energy that come from lasting peace. Consider the techniques he uses to persuade the assembled enemies to try to reach agreement. He cites contrasts in nature and endlessly lists the features of both war and peace, and their relative effects on the use of land and the behaviour of people. He personifies peace as the 'nurse of arts, plenties and joyful births', but shows how all her virtues go to waste and rust in the field during war. It is a moving philosophy. He is really asking the question: what point is there to war when it destroys so much of what the world, its natural resources and its people, have to offer? It is a truly frightening picture of the world, completely in line with the warnings that have been given earlier in the play about the effects of destructive war.

War

'...full accord to all our just demands'

How do you interpret Henry's steadfastness? Moved as he may be by Burgundy's account, he insists that there is to be no compromise. He will bring peace to the country only when his demands are met in full. Is this toughness in keeping with other aspects of Henry's character? Because his main demand is now to marry Katherine, in order to produce an heir to the throne of France, it is important that he and the Princess are left alone in order that he can declare his love and ask her to marry him.

'I have no cunning in protestation...'

Throughout Henry's wooing of Katherine, we learn of yet more qualities to the noble hero. He claims he is a simple soldier, not in possession of the qualities of a lover or courtier. Yet he appears falsely modest, and he is in fact full of quick wit and clever with words. It has been suggested, rather like

Henry V

the practical joke at Agincourt, that he is behaving here once again like his old self, the prince. If you look closely at his patterns of language, a picture emerges of a highly skilled and consciously effective flatterer. He contrasts some of his qualities, he puts himself down, he appears nervous and weak when probably he feels confident and strong, and he asks rhetorical questions. He is sharp with his wits, especially when Katherine wonders how she could possibly love '*de ennemi* of France'. He turns the argument around and claims that in marrying him, she would be marrying the friend of France!

If this is all behaviour mastered self-consciously, does it tell us anything about his other speeches? Has his earlier rhetoric been equally clever? Is he really a character who understands his every move and knows what language to use for each occasion?

'Laissez, laissez!'

Princess Katherine

What about Katherine? Is her modesty genuinely the result of their cultural difference, or is she playing the game of courtship with Henry? Do her exclamations of modesty encourage Henry, or do you think they might have the opposite effect?

Rough tongues

When Burgundy interrupts the wooing he begins a conversation with Henry in which, not for the first time in the play, there is language full of sexual innuendo and smut. This appears as rather a contrast with the tone of Burgundy's earlier language, which was much more statesmanlike. Interestingly, here, Henry readily joins in this banter of bawdy jokes, once again convincing us that his old self may not have been entirely banished from his personality! This sort of moment may have the effect of evoking the character of old Sir John Falstaff, and so, as the audience reaches the end of the epic, there is also a mood of nostalgia.

'The king hath granted every article, His daughter first, and then in sequel al According to their firm proposèd natures'

Princess Katherine

The peace treaty has been framed. The French king consents to Katherine becoming Henry's wife, and it is agreed that Henry will inherit the French throne. Note that the Dauphin, who would have been the expected heir to the throne, is not present in this scene, nor has he appeared in the play for a while. He is now completely disinherited.

Epilogue

What do you make of Chorus' final words? Do you agree with his

Chorus

interpretation that Henry has been 'this star of England'? He tells of what will happen in the future; that Henry VI, the king's and Katherine's son, will lose France and England too will be plunged into a period of civil war. Does this information undermine the achievements of Henry V, who has been a king of such stature? Is fortune now to be considered a stronger influence than it has appeared? Was it simply good fortune that England was blessed with a reformed king and is soon to be disappointed with one who fails? With which other lives has fortune played a part?

Self-test Questions Act 5

Uncover the plot

Delete two of the three alternatives given, to find the correct plot. Beware possible misconceptions and muddles.

Chorus compares Henry's triumphal return after the victory with Alexander's/Caesar's/King Arthur's and then tells how years pass before Henry goes back to France/raises another army/marries. Llewellyn and Pistol continue their conference about mines/argument about being Welsh /joke about women and as a result Pistol is given a present/made to eat a leek/discharged from the army. He laments the death of his wife/the loss of Bardolph/the ending of the wars.

Henry meets the Dauphin/French king/Bourbon and Burgundy is present in order to translate/take possession of French land/negotiate a treaty. Various nobles from both sides leave to discuss terms/drink/play cards and Henry is left to think about the war/write to his nobles/woo Katherine. The French queen also leaves the stage, as it is thought that she will be able to provide refreshments/add a woman's touch to the discussions/seduce the English lords. During his conversation with Katherine, Henry claims that he cannot behave like a courtier/has no money/is feeling ill with the strain of kingship. She wonders whether she really loves him/he will fall in love with another woman/she can possibly love the enemy of France. Hanry talks about their possible dowry/son/old age together. He embarrasses Katherine by describing her appearance/using obscene language during the conversation/kissing her. When he returns, Burgundy makes sexual jokes about Katherine/asks for payment for what he has done/is angry with Henry. A treaty is denied/deferred/agreed and as a result, Henry will marry Katherine/return home empty-handed/give up his lands in Europe.

Chorus tells of the marriage/Henry VI's accession to power/the death of Henry V and also of the loss of France/death of Pistol/defeat of Scotland.

Who? What? Why? When? Where? How?

1 Where do Henry's Lords desire to have him taken?
2 Who brought bread and salt?
3 If Pistol will not eat the leek, what does Llewellyn threaten to do to him?
4 Whose death is lamented?

5 What have grown like savages?
6 Who leaves with the lords to make peace?
7 What does Henry claim he is not very good at?
8 Why doesn't Katherine want to kiss Henry?
9 How do the terms of the treaty help the interests of the English king?
10 What else does the French king grant Henry?

Who said that, and to whom?
1 'St Davy's Day is past'
2 'Bite, I pray you'
3 'Doth fortune play the hussy with me now?'
4 'this day shall change all griefs and quarrels into love'
5 '…all her husbandry doth lie on heaps'
6 '…you must buy that peace
With full accord to all our just demands'
7 'Happily a woman's voice may do some good'
8 'I cannot look greenly, nor gasp out my eloquence'
9 'If you would conjure in her you must make a circle'
10 'And this dear conjunction
Plant neighbourhood and Christian-like accord'

Explain the importance of:
1 The general of the empress.
2 A place where no quarrel could be taken up.
3 A turkey-cock.
4 A groat.
5 Dying vines.
6 Swearing and stern looks.
7 An appointed council.
8 A good heart.
9 A creation with a stubborn outside.
10 Henry VI.

Self-test Answers Act 1

Uncover the plot

Delete two of the three alternatives given, to find the correct plot. Beware possible misconceptions and muddles.

Chorus calls for help from the god of poetry to help present the action of the play. He says that the play will be about a war between two great monarchs and as the war takes place the audience will have to imagine the cavalry moving about the stage.

Canterbury is worried about a proposed law which will strip the Church of its wealth, and when Ely asks him how to prevent it, Canterbury is able to praise the king's goodness. He outlines the ways in which the king has changed and indicates that the Church is willing to support war with France financially. The king asks Canterbury for reasons why the war with France might be just, and Canterbury backs it up with an explanation of the Salic Law, which states that there could be no heir to the French throne from a female line. The king says that they will go to war with France, but must take care of their rear, in order to avoid further danger. Canterbury supports the war effort in a speech comparing the government of the country with honey bees. An ambassador from France arrives with a message from the Dauphin, that the king is still too juvenile. He has also brought a mocking gift. When he receives this, the king retorts with a display of wit. He tells his lords to prepare for war.

Who? What? Why? When? Where? How?

1   The vasty fields of France
2   The helmets from Agincourt
3   Because a bill is planned which will strip the Church of half its possessions.
4   Study, retirement and keeping away from popular places
5   Three French kings have already gained the throne by ignoring the law, there is a flaw in its dating and examples are quoted from the Bible which show that kings can gain a right to the throne from a female line of inheritance.
6   Leave three-quarters of his forces at home
7   He turns the insult to his advantage with a series of puns designed to put the Dauphin in his place
8   He says: 'I will rise there with so full a glory
    That I will dazzle all the eyes of France'
9   God
10 At his (the Dauphin's) father's door

Who said that, and to whom?

1   Canterbury to Ely
2   Canterbury to Ely
3   Ely to Canterbur
4   King Henry to Canterbury
5   Canterbury to the court
6   King Henry to Canterbury
7   Exeter to the king
8   Westmorland to the king
9   Canterbury to the court
10 King Henry to the French messenger

Explain the importance of:

1   The audience is asked by the Chorus to imagine large armies represented by single men

64

2   The audience is asked by the Chorus to imagine long time periods, of many years, compressed into an hour-glass

3   At this point, the king's (Henry V's) wildness also 'died'

4   This is the image used by Ely to describe Henry's reformation

5   Canterbury argues that one of the reasons why the Salic law is irrelevant is because the land is in Germany, and not France

6   Edward the Black Prince defeated the French (actually in 1346 at Crécy)

7   An image used by the king to describe the way that the Scots have invaded England in the past

8   Canterbury builds a theory of harmonious and diverse political life around the metaphor of the honey bees

9   The messenger insults the king by saying that he cannot hope to win the lands of France by dancing

10   The insult of the gift of tennis balls is revealed

Self-test Answers Act 2

Uncover the plot

Delete two of the three alternatives given, to find the correct plot. Beware possible misconceptions and muddles.

Nym is angry that Nell Quickly is married and as a result he insults Pistol. The Boy tells the other characters from the tavern that their old friend Falstaff is very ill. They regret that Falstaff has had his heart broken.

Meanwhile, the king faces a problem. Cambridge, Scroop and Gray have become traitors and they must be sentenced accordingly. Before he punishes them, Henry agrees to pardon another man. When he speaks to the three men he compares their actions to the work of the devil, and so he sentences them to death.

As Falstaff's death is described, we hear that he cried out against drink, and the Boy also describes the way that he spoke out against women. As Pistol is about to leave for France he advises the Hostess, his wife, to look after his belongings. In the king's palace at Rouen, the French king orders the defence of French towns. The Dauphin assumes that England still has an idle kIng, and so he is not worried. However, the Constable reports that Henry has changed. Exeter arrives in France and demands that the French king give up the lands that belong by right to England. If the French refuse, Exeter says that there will be a bloody war. There is another message, a personal one for the Dauphin, whom King Henry personally dislikes. The Dauphin says that he presented Henry with the tennis balls, intending to make a mocking statement about Henry's youth. Exeter tells the French that the English have already landed in France.

Who? What? Why? When? Where? How?

1   Nell Quickly

2   They sheathe their swords and make peace between each other

3   Because Sir John Falstaff is dying

4   By flattering them

5   They find him too lenient

6   Lord Scroop

7   Falstaff – on his deathbed, as he was delirious

8   King Henry, by the Dauphin

9   The next day

10   He has changed: he now never wastes his time any longer

Who said that, and to whom?
1 Chorus speaks these words
2 Pistol to Nym
3 The Hostess, about Falstaff, to Pistol, Nym and Bardolph
4 Scroop to the king
5 The king to Scroop
6 The king to the conspirators
7 Gray to the king
8 The Boy, about Falstaff, to the other tavern characters
9 The Dauphin to the French king
10 Exeter to the French king

Explain the importance of:
1 Chorus describes the enthusiastic preparations for the war effort in England
2 Pistol and Nym come close to fighting
3 Pistol says that Falstaff's heart has been broken by the king
4 King Henry gives Cambridge, Scroop and Gray their indictments and they then confess
5 This is what Henry compares the conspiracy with
6 The Hostess is muddled – she means to say that Falstaff is in *Abraham's bosom*, not Arthur's, a mythical British king
7 Pistol encourages his friends to go to war with France for personal profit
8 The French king orders his lords to defend various towns in the path of the English advance
9 The French king recalls the French being defeated at Crécy, at the hands of the Black Prince
10 This is the Dauphin, who has a personal dislike of King Henry

Self-test answers Act 3

Uncover the plot
Chorus describes the departure of the English troops for Harfleur and explains that a treaty is proposed by the French involving the offer of marriage to Princess Katherine. The king persuades his troops to fight in the siege of Harfleur by imitating a tiger, but this has little effect on Pistol and Nym, who spend their time singing instead of going forward. The Boy is disgusted by their cowardice. Llewellyn and MacMorris discuss the mining. After the siege, the king demands that the Governor submits. If there is no agreement, Henry says that he will not be responsible for his soldiers' actions.

Whilst learning some English words, Princess Katherine discovers that some of the words sound rude. The French nobles are surprised at the English advances and insult England. They think of the English climate as damp and the ale as weak. The Constable is sure that, when he sees the French army, King Henry will want to offer a ransom.

Whilst defending the bridge at Ternoise, Pistol convinces Llewellyn that he is a brave soldier, but Llewellyn is later told the truth by Gower. Bardolph is sentenced to hang because he has stolen a crucifix. Montjoy arrives to negotiate a ransom but Henry stands firm. During the night before the battle, Bourbon brags about his horse before he and other French nobles start to make rude jokes. The French noblemen mock the English and compare their soldiers to dogs.

Who? What? Why? When? Where? How?
1   Some petty and unprofitable dukedoms
2   Their mothers
3   They are cowards
4   MacMorris
5   They will no longer be under control
6   That some of the words sound like rude French words
7   He thinks that Pistol is a brave soldier
8   Calais
9   That the English will fight on
10 It is full of sexual innuendo

Who said that, and to whom?
1   The king, to his troops at Harfleur
2   The king, to his troops at Harfleur
3   Nym, to Pistol and Bardolph
4   MacMorris to Llewellyn
5   The Governor of Harfleur, to the king
6   Dauphin to the French nobles
7   Llewellyn to Pistol
8   The king to Llewellyn, about Bardolph
9   Orléans to Bourbon
10 Orléans to the French lords

Explain the importance of:
1   The French king's daughter, Katherine, is offered as a means of preventing the war
2   The image used by Henry to describe his men at Harfleur
3   This is what the Boy has to say about Bardolph
4   These are the mines which Llewellyn criticises
5   The image that Henry uses to describe his troops if Harfleur is not surrendered
6   Katherine learns these English words
7   As the French mock the English, they describe some of their dances
8   The crucifix stolen by Bardolph
9   Exeter maintains defence of the bridge at Ternoise
10 Henry says it is the air of France which causes him to brag

Self-test Answers Act 4

Uncover the plot
Delete two of the three alternatives given, to find the correct plot. Beware possible misconceptions and muddles.

Chorus describes the two armies during the night before the battle. The French play at dice to pass the time, whilst the English sit and wait patiently. Henry borrows a cloak from Sir Thomas Erpingham and goes amongst his men. He first meets Pistol, who says that the king is a good man. Henry thinks about the problems of kingship and talks about the trappings of ceremony. He envies the peasants, who do not have the burden of kingship to face up to.

As the French prepare for battle, they think of the English as easy prey and offer to send them dinners. In answer to Westmorland's anxieties, the king encourages his troops to go into battle by telling them that they are lucky to be part of his brotherhood. When Montjoy arrives for one final demand of a ransom, Henry tells him that he will fight to the end. Pistol does take a ransom of two hundred crowns, from his French prisoner. After the victory, Henry is made angry by the murder of the luggage boys, and in retaliation he orders the death of all prisoners.

Earlier, before the battle, the king has given Williams his glove and looks forward to meeting him again to finish an argument. After the battle he fools Llewellyn into thinking that Williams is a traitor, but prevents any further conflict and gives Williams some money.

Who? What? Why? When? Where? How?

1   Sir Thomas Erpingham's
2   Cornwall
3   They are making too much noise
4   Without redemption
5   Five hundred
6   It is St Crispin's Day
7   His body
8   Nym and Bardolph
9   Henry's glove
10 Hymns and psalms of praise

Who said that, and to whom?

1   Chorus
2   Chorus
3   The king to Williams
4   Williams to the king
5   Constable to the French troops
6   The king to his men
7   Pistol to the French prisoner
8   Llewellyn to Gower
9   The king to Llewellyn
10 Williams to Llewellyn

Explain the importance of:

1   A rude sign from Pistol to the king
2   The king and Williams exchange gloves in order to recognise each other to continue their argument
3   The king reflects on 'idol ceremony' when he thinks about the nature of kingship
4   An image used by Grandpré for the English horsemen
5   Henry tells his men that they will not forget the battle
6   Part of the image used by the Boy to describe Pistol
7   The feeling of the French as the battle is lost
8   The Welsh river that Llewellyn compares to the river in Macedon
9   The king tells Llewellyn that the glove he gives him came from a French lord and that any challenger is a traitor
10 The total of French casualties

Self-test Answers Act 5

Uncover the plot

Delete two of the three alternatives given, to find the correct plot. Beware possible misconceptions and muddles.

Chorus compares Henry's triumphal return after the victory with Caesar's and then tells how years pass before Henry goes back to France. Llewellyn and Pistol continue their argument about being Welsh and as a result Pistol is made to eat a leek. He laments the death of his wife.

Henry meets the French king and Burgundy is present in order to negotiate a treaty. Various nobles from both sides leave to discuss terms and Henry is left to woo Katherine. The French queen also leaves the stage, as it is thought that she will be able to add a woman's touch to the discussions. During his conversation with Katherine, Henry claims that he cannot behave like a courtier. She wonders whether she can possibly love the enemy of France. Henry talks about their possible son. He embarrasses Katherine by kissing her. When he returns, Burgundy makes sexual jokes about Katherine. A treaty is agreed and as a result, Henry will marry Katherine.

Chorus tells of Henry VI's accession to power and also of the loss of France.

Who? What? Why? When? Where? How?
1 Blackheath
2 Pistol
3 Beat him about the head for days
4 Doll's
5 The sciences, during the war
6 The French queen
7 Courtship
8 It is not the French fashion
9 His son will be heir to the French throne
10 His daughter's hand in marriage

Who said that, and to whom?
1 Gower to Llewellyn
2 Llewellyn to Pistol
3 Pistol, on his own
4 The French queen to Henry
5 Burgundy to all in the French court
6 Henry to the French court
7 The French queen to the French king
8 Henry to Katherine
9 Burgundy to Henry
10 The French king to Henry

Explain the importance of:
1 The Earl of Essex, a contemporary reference
2 Llewellyn was insulted when he could not quarrel with Pistol
3 Gower's image to describe Pistol
4 Money given to Pistol by Llewellyn to ease his pains
5 One of Burgundy's images to describe the effects of war on France
6 Burgundy says that this is what people are driven to in times of war
7 The lords who will withdraw to negotiate the peace treaty
8 In his wooing, Henry says this will remain constant
9 Henry's description, to Katherine, of himself
10 Henry's son, who lost France and allowed civil war to develop in England

■ Writing an examination essay

Take the following to heart
- *Carefully study each of the questions set on a particular text* Make sure you understand what they are asking for so that you select the one you know most about.
- *Answer the question* Obvious, isn't it? But bitter experience shows that many students fail because they do not actually answer the question that has been set.
- *Answer all the question* Again, obvious, but so many students spend all their time answering just part of a question and ignoring the rest. This prevents you gaining marks for the parts left out.

The question
1 Read and understand every word of it. If it asks you to compare (the similarities) and/or contrast (the differences) between characters or events, then that is what you must do.
2 Underline all the key words and phrases that mention characters, events and themes, and all instructions as to what to do, e.g. compare, contrast, outline, comment, give an account, write about, show how/what/where.
3 Now write a short list of the things you have to do, one item under the other. A typical question will only have between two and five items at most for you to cope with.

Planning your answer
1 Look at each of the points you have identified from the question. Think about what you are going to say about each. Much of it will be pretty obvious, but if you think of any good ideas, jot them down before you forget them.
2 Decide in what order you are going to deal with the question's major points. Number them in sequence.
3 So far you have done some concentrated, thoughtful reading and written down maybe fifteen to twenty words. You know roughly what you are going to say in response to the question and in what order – if you do not, you have time to give serious thought to trying one of the other questions.

Putting pen to paper
The first sentences are important. Try to summarise your response to the question so the examiner has some idea of how you are going to approach it. Do not say 'I am going to write about the character of Macbeth and show how evil he was' but instead write 'Macbeth was a weak-willed, vicious traitor. Totally dominated by his "fiend-like queen", he deserved the epitaph "this dead butcher" – or did he?' Jump straight into the essay, do not nibble at its extremities for a page and a half. High marks will be gained by the candidate who can show he or she has a mind engaged with the text. Your personal response is rewarded – provided you are answering the question!

As you write your essay *constantly refer back to your list of points* and make sure you are actually responding to them.

How long should it be?
There is no 'correct' length. What you must do is answer the question set, fully and sensitively, in the time allowed. Allocate time to each question according to the percentage of marks awarded for it.

How much quotation or paraphrase?
Use only that which is relevant and contributes to the quality and clarity of your answer. Padding is a waste of your time and gains not a single mark.